Art & Science of Coaching

Step-by-Step Coaching

Marilyn W. Atkinson, Ph.D., and Rae T. Chois

Art & Science of Coaching: Step-by-Step Coaching

Copyright © 2010 by Exalon Publishing, LTD

All rights reserved. No portion of this book may be reproduced, by any process or technique, without the express written consent of the publisher.

ISBN-978-0-9783704-5-9

First published in 2007.

Printed in the United States of America.

The paper used in this book complies with the Permanent Paper Standard issued by the National Information Standards Organization (Z39,48-1984).

10 9 8 7 6 5 4 3 2 1

Dedication

We dedicate this book to the Spirit of Milton Erickson. His love of inquiry and compassionate appreciation of people and their abilities has inspired me for a lifetime.

Marilyn W. Atkinson, Ph.D.

An Acknowledgment

For every powerful creation requiring commitment and development over months and years there is usually a strong team. The *Art & Science of Coaching* as a trilogy of three books, was written over two years, with two committed people juggling between multiple coach training programs, clients, and other human development projects on four continents. These books have taken tag team efforts and earnest conversations between Marilyn W. Atkinson, Ph.D., and Rae T. Chois, ICF Master Certified Coach, crossing many countries where courses were being given and coaching conversations being had.

The supportive team that assisted during this effort provided enthusiasm and excitement, but also strong critical editorial know-how. It took a truly committed team to finish the three books. Rae T. Chois created the first tangible draft and outline of the *Art & Science of Coaching* series. Rae challenged me, the principal author, about timing to complete, as well as adding her ongoing writing, content, and editorial capacities at every stage. It was a fun adventure with Rae as together we put these powerful concepts into writing. Ideas in this series originated from many sources. Special appreciation goes to Robert Dilts who added so much to our lives with his Logical Levels model.

A group of coaches and authors became early editing readers. Thank you to Ann Hazelquist, Cheryl Hughes, Bonnie Beriault, Lisa Hepner, Cari Beckett, Larrye Heyl and Heather Parks. They provided useful proofing commentaries and strong readership suggestions. Several trainers, including Richard Hyams of Vancouver, Benjamin Schulman of Moscow, and Stanislav Grindberg of Ekaterinburg, provided exercises and ideas. My spouse, Lawrence McGinnis, provided hours of patient review, conversation about elements, and more editorial assistance to make the work flow, month by month. Rae's children Isaieh and Jos also generously gave up their time with their mom. Thanks to the Chois boys!

Coaches around the world, including Anna Lebedeva, Maxim Oshurkov, and Sveta Chumakova in Russia, Ekaterina Druzhinina in Ukraine, and Eser Buyukaydin and Zerrin Baser in Turkey, have provided strong, enthusiastic support at every stage. They quickly translated the books into two more languages, Russian and Turkish.

Also, thank you to all the amazing trainers and coach mentors who have supported the development of Erickson's ICF Accredited Coach Training program called the *Art & Science of Coaching* through time including (but not limited to) Richard Hyams, Lori-anne Demers, Thomi Glover, Tony Husted, Kathy McKenzie, Jan Georg Kristiansen, Hanna Sedal, Anna Lebedeva, Maxim Oshurkov, Sveta Chumakova, Katya Maximova, Raisa Belousova, Sergei Kapitsa, Janet Soyak, Eser Buyukaydin, Zerrin Baser, Svetlana Popova, Stanislav Grindberg, Teresia LaRocque, Linda Hamilton, Jiri Kunkar, and Barry Switnicki.

A team of editors, publishers, copy editors, and typists, including Kazim Sari, Teoman Akben, and Laura Poole, as well as Beverley Handren and Carol Dale, kept the drafts in order, the structures clean, and the work progressing. Elif Berna Kutluata worked hard on Turkish editing. Kathleen O'Brien polished the chapters. Fiona Nicholson and Vanessa Husted provided diagrams and images book by book.

Also, thank you to all other Erickson staff and trainers from every country across the globe. It is through your efforts that this material reaches the minds and hearts of so many people.

An Acknowledgment

How does one truly acknowledge such a team? Only by having this result be a landmark and a well-used celebration of their time, energy, and commitment.

I send you all blessings and deep gratitude for your support.

Marilyn W. Atkinson, Ph.D.
November 2007

Contents

Dedication i

An Acknowledgment iii

List of Figures xiii

Introduction xv
    This Book's Purpose xv
    Getting the Most From This Book xviii

1   **Building Rapport to Start Building Relationships** 1
    Rapport and Transformational Conversations 4
    People Like People Who Are Like Themselves 4
    Finding Common Ground to Lead to Successful Results 5
    The Important R Skills that Lead to Successful Results 7
    Deeper Relationships: Shared Interests and Values 8
    Four Tools for Impactful Communication 10
    Tool One: Verbal Softeners 10
    Tool Two: The Fine Art of Backtracking 12
    Tool Three: Naming the Outcome in Advance 14
    Tool Four: Stepping into the Generous Space
        of Coach Position 14
    The Rapport Wheel Exercise 18

2 The "Sound" of Powerful Listening 21

Listening Through and For Values 22
Provide an Envelope for Listening 24
On What Level Do You Tend to Listen?................. 25
Level 1 Listening: Content Listening 25
Level 2 Listening: Context, Structure, and
    Process Listening 27
Listening for Competence Gives Form to Inner Resources 28
Level 3 Listening: Global, Contextual, and
    Form Listening 31
The "Big Ears" Exercise 34

3 Questioning versus Telling: The Advice-Free Zone 37

Moving Beyond Internal Dialogue Repetition 38
Questions: The Royal Road to Self-Discovery
    and Skill Discovery 40
Taking Charge of a Project:
    The Process of Self-Evaluation 42
An Important Distinction: How versus Why 43
The Future Focus: The Why of Importance 44
Brainstorming without Telling:
    The Chinese Menu Approach 46
Coaching Example 47
An Example of Powerful Questions:
    Scaling to Create Momentum 48
Types of Scaling Questions 49
Action Steps 49
Commitment 50
Confidence 50
Effectiveness with Results 50
Motivation 51
Satisfaction 52
Comfort 53
Fulfillment 53

Milestones 53
Priority 53
Risk 54

4 Turning on the Tap: The Magic of Open-Ended Questions 59

The Nature of Great Questions 61
The Power of Open-Ended Questions 62
Open-Ended versus Closed Questions 63
The Tone of Open-Ended Questions 64
Opening Out: Discovering Choices 65
Making Open-Ended Questions Even More Open-Ended .. 66
The Open-Ended Line Exercise 71
Powerful Questions from Coach Position 75

5 The Secret Tones of Transformation 77

Using Your Coaching Voice for Maximum Impact 80
Cultivating a Range of Tones 81
Open-Ended Tone 1: The Tone of the Wizard 82
Practice Phrases 82
Open-Ended Tone 2: The Tone of the True Friend 83
Practice Phrases 84
Open-Ended Tone 3: The Tone of the Visionary Elder 85
Practice Phrases 86
Exercise: Cultivating a Range of Open-Ended Tones 87
The Closed Tone: The Tone of the Warrior 88
Examples 89

6 The Power of Framing and Committing 93

Outcome Thinking 97
Find Elegant Solutions to Problems 98
The Key Skill that Makes the Difference
  in Transformational Communication 101

7 Contracting: Setting the Focus of the Conversation 105

- The Power of Contracts 109
- Contracting Sets the Intention and Attention
  of Powerful Coaching 109
- Using the Contracting Question to Set the Focus 110
- From Abstract to Specific:
  50,000-Feet Contracts to 50-Feet Contracts 112
- Effective Contracting Considerations 113
- Listening for a Creator, Reactor, or Visitor 114
- Visitors 116
- Reactors 117
- Creators 118
- The Five Criteria of a Good Contract 119
- Complaining Pattern Awareness 120

8 The Four Essential Questions in Coaching 123

- The Power of Full Intention to Bring Us to Full Value ... 125
- The Personal Reach Exercise 126
- "Flow" Conversations: A Fluid Model 127
- Questions Are the Answer 128
- Four Engaging Questions
  That Support the Unfolding of Any Project 129
- Question 1: What Do You Want? 130
- Question 2: How Might You Get It? 132
- Question 3: How Might You Deepen Your Commitment? 134
- The I.A.M. Formula
  Intention + Attention = Masterful Manifestation 136
- Question 4: How Will You Know You've Got It? 137

9 Designing Your Dream: The Outcome Frame 139

- What Is the Outcome Frame? 142
- Stated in the Positive 143

In the Person's Control 145
Is the Goal SMART? 148
Is the Goal Ecological? 150
Valuable Approaches for Developing Futures 151
Dissociated versus Associated Experience 151
Key Points for Coaching 153

10 Inner Alignment with Logical Levels 161

Value Design Forms through Logical Levels Questions . 162
Misaligned Logic in the Success Recipe 163
Logical Levels of the Mind 164
Questions for Transformational Conversations:
    The Logical Levels Pattern from the Top Down 165
How Does It Work Operationally? 168
The Central "Why" Question: Integrity Organization 169
The Logical Level Benefits 170
Using Logical Levels: Coach Benefits 173
Logical Levels and Organizational Hierarchy 173
Logical Levels: Focus and Outcome Summary 175
Behavior and Identity Confusion 178
Coaching Conversations that Use Logical Levels
    with the Outcome Frame 180
The Logical Level Coaching Worksheet 182
Audio Exercise: Structural Listening 183

11 Amazing Grace: Taking Action and Completing the Conversation 185

The Language of Taking Action 190
Total Session Progression: Open-Ended to Closed 191
The Tone of Action Language 193
Action Language That Compels 193
Alternate Approaches if the Action Plan Is Delayed 196
Approaching Closure: The Where and the When 197
Final Footprints:
    Debriefing the Value of the Conversation 198

The Final Acknowledgment by the Coach 200
Exercise: The Logical Levels Acknowledgment 201
The Exercise 202

12 The Self-Examined Communicator 207

The Nature of Self-Trust:
Aligning with Your Vision and Your Mission 211
Human Complexity and Dynamic Emergence 214
Awakened Awareness, Self-Knowledge, and Listening .. 214
Beyond Bias: The Advantage of Allowing 215
Advancing Your Skill Development Through Time 216
Aligning with Vision: The Use of Overlap Language 217
A Picture Can Speak More than 1000 Words 218
Integrating the Science of Inner Processing 219

13 Overview of Transformational Conversations Using the Solution-Focused Coach Approach 221

Contract (Session Topic/Focus) 222
Coach Explores Outcome Planning Steps and Questions 222
Fieldwork and Design of Effective Actions 223
Person Asked to Debrief
How the Session Was Most Useful to Them 223
Coach Completes by Acknowledging and
Sharing Heartfelt Appreciation for Client 224
A 15-Minute Coaching Session with Lucy 224
A 25-Minute Coaching Session with Emma 228

Continue to Explore Art & Science of Coaching 239

Meet the Authors 241

Suggested Readings 245

Erickson College International Locations ... 249

List of Figures

Rapport and Relationships 18

Example Rapport Wheel 19

Five Erickson Principles 29

The Open-Ended Line 66

Four Creative Tones Functions 91

Four Stages of a Plan and Fulfillment 129

The Four Planning Questions in the Quadrant Model 138

The Logical Levels 168

Second Tier of Logical Levels 179

Logical Levels with the Outcome Frame 183

Logical Levels 204

Introduction

This Book's Purpose

We, two Erickson College trainers, Marilyn Atkinson and Rae T. Chois, are proud to present Book Two in the series *Art & Science of Coaching* called *Step-by-Step Coaching*. This is the book many having been waiting for, and it details and clarifies the "what to do and how to do it" of effective coaching and transformational conversations.

Book One, *Inner Dynamics,* provided a strong framework and vantage point for thinking about coaching as a human development vehicle, and gave some exercises and processes for understanding the power of coaching for people in the 21st Century. It offered a way to think about mind-brain use and the nature of integrative thinking (so we can use coaching to build this integrity). It showed the four key aspects of any project and how they give us essential springboards for moving beyond "gremlin" thinking in our projects. In Book One, we also introduced some powerful maps, four-quadrant visuals placed on a diamond, to assist these key understandings of the macro elements of the coaching vision and aim.

This second book offers skill development practice with the coaching arrow, a metaphor for clarifying and detailing an effective coaching conversation. In the same way as the diamond from Book One assisted with understanding the macro elements, the coaching arrow in Book Two assists the reader to detail and sequence the micro elements of an effective coaching conversation. Following elements of the arrow opens the path and directs the reader through the book as the arrow highlights a clear unfolding of an effective coaching conversation. Informed by the frameworks of the diamond and the arrow, a coach has an overview whereby he or she can design the most useful next step in the conversation.

Even though it is detailed, the arrow framework is only an introduction to the basic structure of a coaching conversation. Every coaching conversation is unique as people become empowered in wonderfully unique ways. Strong solution focused coaches use a combination of coaching processes (transformational recipes for empowerment developed by studying the nature of the mind) and coaching tools (step-by-step questioning frameworks that assist a person to move quickly to the heart of an important choice or discovery). This second book focuses in the second area, the steps of effective coaching questions and solution- focused tools. (Our next book, Book Three, is about coaching processes.)

Tools are a fascinating area in coaching as they take us right to the heart of the thinking process itself. We are stepping into a design function of questions that may seem simple but in fact offer amazing variations in application. Viewing the valleys and mountains of the mind, distinguish between 5,000-foot conversations and 50-foot conversations. Because of that variety in our human styles and responses, the book will give you just a taste of the powerful quality of real coaching applications. The book, in fact, makes available perhaps 10 percent of the coaching tools you would learn in an Art and Science of Coaching, Erickson training program.

To provide even 10 percent requires a smorgasbord of examples that cover many areas and provide a real opportunity for mastery. In this book we also provide visual maps and verbal reviews of actual coaching sessions. We are pleased with the detail level because we want to support you, our readers, in diving in fully and engaging with the coaching arrow.

Our primary aim is that through the practice and exercises with sound examples you will develop a strong incentive to explore the practice of coaching on a daily basis. We introduce key distinctions so that you get an overview and perspective, as well as a taste and a feel for the elements of transformational conversations in all areas of life. A warning however: Many reviewers have become sufficiently intrigued by even this taste that they put themselves in the first available live program of the Art and Science of Coaching. Once people get into the heart of this work they realize it is much more effective to learn about transformational coaching by doing it than reading about it or talking about it.

Our second aim in including the step-by-step practice was to provide readers with an interactive journey that powerfully introduces you to understanding the linkage between key foundational elements in all transformational discovery systems. Participate in the individual and paired practice and you will begin to develop a foundation rooted in today's most current and powerful communicating and relating theories. As you practice coaching using these tools, your life will be enriched from the inside out.

When you arrive at the end of this book, know that you have completed the first step in gaining a solid foundation in what we, our colleagues, and Erickson College graduates consider to be one of life's most important skill sets. In fact, we believe that these communication skills provide participants with true understanding of integral change such that we can literally transform the globe, one conversation at a time.

Getting the Most From This Book

To get the most out of this book, we encourage the following.

1. **Try out the coaching exercises and methodologies in this book.** Erickson College's methodologies and coaching systems are known by our international graduates to be very powerful and transformational, and we strongly encourage you to complete the coaching exercises and methodologies in this book.

2. **Do not believe a word in this book. Prove the concepts for yourself!** Explore these tools and practice them so you integrate them fully into your life, and you will find yourself moving forward powerfully toward a fully satisfying and successful life. In other words, do not blindly believe a word in this book, but try the concepts and exercises. Prove them for yourself! We also encourage you to work with an Erickson-trained coach, if at all possible, as they are trained to use these tools and many more.

3. **Have a beginner's mind.** We request that you go through this book holding and maintaining a beginner's mind. Read each chapter as if you are a curious scientist looking at life in a new and profound way. As you bring *all of yourself* to each chapter—all your past learning, insights, frustrations, etc.—while recognizing and honoring each of the stages of development you have passed through previously, you will find rewarding insights and self-discovery approaches to move to your own next stage in your journey. If you participate fully, you will find the experience of reading this book tremendously useful to your life both as client and coach.

4   **Enjoy all the stages of learning.** To learn anything in life, there are four phases that you will consistently go through. The same will likely be true as you experience practicing the steps of transformational conversations as described in this book. You will be thinking and framing ideas, planning and asking creative questions, and working in a way that may be very different than your prior way of thinking made possible. Take a moment to plan your steps, passing through these four phases as you gain competence with this book's advanced skill set.

- **Stage 1: Unconscious incompetence**
  The stage of unconscious incompetence is when you are not aware that you don't know how to do something. In this stage you will awaken to what you "don't-know-that-you-don't-know" as you begin to practice for the first time.

- **Stage 2: Conscious incompetence**
  In this stage, you begin to practice the new skill you want to learn but know that you are not yet very proficient. For most of us, this phase is very challenging as most people finding it difficult to learn by making mistakes! This phase often leads to some real resistance. This resistance forces many well-intentioned people to quit at the stage of conscious incompetence. You will learn a great deal of information at a very rapid pace.

- **Stage 3: Conscious competence**
  This is where you have started to develop a skill, but it is not yet integrated, consistent, or habitual. In this phase you still need to concentrate and direct your energy. Step by step you notice you can do it, and your skill and confidence grows.

- **Stage 4: Unconscious competence**
  At this stage, the skills and this new way of relating become habitual and automatic for you. Your conscious mind can focus on others things while you naturally and easily demonstrate the skill and this new way of being. As a driver you are able to carry on a conversation, plan your day, and make your way to your destination, all while competently driving.

Most people think of the stage of unconscious competence as the stage of mastery, and yet consider that a real master never considers himself or herself a master. A real master retains a beginner's mind, is committed to waking up to what he or she doesn't know that he or she doesn't know (unconscious incompetence), and is committed to learning more, going deeper into the study of their subject. In fact, consider that the phrase "I already know that" stops you from being available for new learning. Making mastery focus a central part of your life accelerates your growth, development, and flourishing as a human being.

5 **Take your time and savor the practices in this book slowly as you engage authentically with others.** Coaching is about truly coming to know ourselves and each other. The practice of solution-focused coaching leads to deep awareness of the subtle elements of human development. To savor this is to taste the best wine from the vineyard of each others lives.

CHAPTER 1

Building Rapport to Start Building Relationships

And I strive to discover how to signal my companions . . . to say in time a simple word, a password like conspirators. Let us unite. Let us hold each other tightly, let us merge our hearts, let us create for Earth a brain and a heart.

—Nikos Kazantzakis

Shall we dance?

—The King and I

The Story of Milton and George

*A*s a young psychiatrist, Milton Erickson worked with patients in mental hospitals. He once described his interactions with a man named George who spoke "word salad," a mixture of multiple mixed phrases, nouns, and verbs in no clear order. Milton met George on his first day of work on the back wards at the Worcester State Mental Hospital in New York in the late 1920s. George had been picked up from a back road, where he had been found wandering aimlessly five years before. No one knew his last name or background because he only spoke word salad. Only his name, George, identified him.

Milton's first meeting with George startled him. As Milton toured a ward for the first time, George, who had been sitting passively on a bench, suddenly jumped up, ran toward Milton, and for about two minutes spoke word salad in an excited tone of voice! The nurses explained that he only did this when a new person came into the ward.

Milton listened with interest, and then came back with his secretary, an expert in shorthand. She wrote down George's words as he spoke them at Milton's second visit. Then Milton spent several weeks developing a word salad of his own and practicing it privately. He had an idea, and fully implementing it required practice and commitment.

When he was finally ready, Milton once again went to the ward. George jumped up, came forward, and spoke three sentences of excited word salad. Milton responded with three sentences of equally enthusiastic word salad. George seemed astounded. He sat on the bench and eyed Milton with interest. Milton also sat down and waited.

After ten minutes of thought, George stood up and started pacing up and down beside Milton, speaking methodically in word salad. It was as if he was telling a reasonable story, and he spoke for ten minutes.

CHAPTER 1 *Building Rapport to Start Building Relationships*

When he was done, he sat on the bench. Milton stood up, and for ten minutes paced up and down and responded to George with methodical, reasoned word salad. He, too, sat down on the bench.

Fifteen minutes later, another round began. George stood up and, with many gestures and with much more passion in his voice, started a monologue in word salad for half an hour. This time it was as if he was telling Milton his authentic feelings about life. Bringing his feelings totally into the word salad, he sometimes sounded sad, sometimes angry, sometimes excited. Milton listened carefully to the total expression, and when it was his turn, he also spoke for a similar period. Like an orchestral refrain, he brought the whole emotional range into his voice as well. When he was complete, he sat down. George, who had been calmly sitting on the bench watching, nodded gravely. They were now in true rapport. George was noticeably moved and also more relaxed.

"Speak sense, Doctor," George said.

"I will," responded Milton. "Tell me, what is your last name?"

George spoke two sentences of word salad and then said his last name. Milton responded with two sentences of word salad, and asked, "Where are you from?"

Within half an hour, Milton got George's whole history. Over the next few months George became a changed man. At first he only talked with Milton, but gradually, over the months he made more understandable communication with others. He began to speak in responsible ways and started doing small jobs for the nurses. Soon he was outside, working on the grounds.

On checking his history, Milton discovered that George's family was dead and he had recently inherited a small farm. About eleven months after Milton's first talk with him, George was capable of returning to his farm. He lived there for the rest of his life, and for forty years

3

maintained yearly communication by postcard with Milton. His messages were cryptic: "Built a new roof on the barn this winter." Or "15 new lambs; all in good shape." Then he would sign his name and finish his postcard with two sentences of word salad.

Rapport and Transformational Conversations

Transformational conversations are the means by which you help yourself and others become aligned and purposeful humans. They are the way through which we, as humans, express and live from our inner truth while supporting others in doing the same. Rapport is at the heart of these conversations.

The word *rappoarte* comes from the Greek language, and means "to carry back to another person an experience of themselves." The story of Milton Erickson and George is a good example of effective rapport in action.

People Like People Who Are Like Themselves

Rapport building is being willing to understand or experience another person's view of the world as if you were that person. If you were to know what a person knows, have experienced what he or she has experienced, and want what he or she wants, you would be able to naturally enter into this person's physical and tonal habits and world view. Because it is not possible to entirely walk in someone's shoes, strong communicators build rapport through a willingness to understand and respect another person's model of the world. The key is to honor the person by finding the common ground, which leads to successful results by asking powerful questions and by listening with curiosity and respect.

The deeper mind looks for understanding before it offers its wisdom into any conversation. Building rapport with a person—stepping into his or her world—is the easiest and fastest way of communicating with the deeper mind.

Your emotional brain loves *sameness*. It feels safe and most comfortable when communicating with people who are *like* you, who are considered part of your tribe or family. You can encourage a person's emotional brain to relax and be open to a transformational conversation by using the basic skills of rapport in any conversation. You will be building a sense of shared value with the person so that client will step into relationship with you.

Without rapport, an effective coaching conversation cannot happen. A person must feel safe and understood to open up to deeper meaning. We have transformational conversations with people we value!

Finding Common Ground to Lead to Successful Results

When you deepen your understanding of a person's world through a strong commitment to listen, understand, and communicate, it's as if you *are* the person. The more you are the person, the deeper your understanding and respect for his or her world. The deeper the rapport, the more the person feels respected and understood. All of this means that there is a greater opportunity for a transformational conversation to happen.

We use behavioral and tonal matching to develop strong physical rapport. With behavioral matching, you adopt part of a person's behavior. For instance, in a person-to-person conversation, you might sit in the same posture as the person. When the person strongly shifts positions, you gradually and gracefully follow. If they have very straight posture, you straighten up to sense their inner way of being. This is a form of respect, and it eases the ability to truly listen to the person.

Rapport is an elegant dance. It is very important to realize that rapport building is not about copying the person or mimicking behavior. If a person feels copied, they might feel you are mocking them, which dramatically breaks rapport. Rapport starts when we quietly track the person's behavior and begin the dance of sharing their world of experience. Being "like them" is the doorway into sharing experience.

When you go for a hike with someone, he or she is more comfortable if you walk at his or her speed rather than if you walk much faster or much slower. To build rapport, you respond to the walking pattern by walking at the same pace. You may not walk exactly like the person, but when you move at the same pace, it creates relaxation and a sense of partnership that leads to effective conversation. He feels more comfortable, and gradually a flow of shared meanings and shared values develops between both of you. Then you can invite him to quicken or change pace, and he will be more likely to agree.

Pacing is the gradual process of gaining rapport. Just as you pace someone when you walk to match hiking speed, you pace a person as you build rapport. The term *pace* in Old Latin means to "be at peace with." As rapport is built and increased, you have the opportunity to lead the person with effective questions. When enough rapport has been built and you gently relax, the client will naturally relax with you. This can be a very useful way to gracefully lead a person out of a disempowering state and into a more resourceful one.

Your emotions follow your body, just as your body leads your emotions. This is the old chicken or egg syndrome—which came first? By gaining rapport and then leading the person into new expressions, you have the opportunity to assist someone in accessing more empowering emotions, resources, and states of mind.

Here is a rapport-building exercise to try. Practice matching your breathing to another person until you get a sense of his or her rhythm. If the person seems rather dissociated or disjointed, you might start to slowly deepen your breathing and notice if the other person starts to deepen his or hers as well. Usually a person will do so, unconsciously responding to you. This will enhance contact and will also assist the person to touch deeper levels of awareness. If you relax, the person will relax, too. He will particularly appreciate you after this type of relaxation, although he may not consciously recognize what you have done.

The Important R Skills that Lead to Successful Results

We notice *results* when we build *relationships* and amplify *respect* through the process of *rapport*. A very important aspect of respectful listening is the process of matching voice tone and tempo. It is sometimes useful for the first few minutes of a coaching conversation to step into the person's shoes as if you could be them momentarily. Listen to tone, tempo, and volume of voice and bring yourself to that quality of vocal expression. Do this almost as if you were a tape recorder, matching the speaker's tempo and rhythm. Like Milton with George, be as alert as possible to changes in expression, and respond to them.

Tone of voice is very important to humans. Think of someone you do not particularly respect, and think about their voice, listening to it inwardly. You will notice that their voice is not at all like yours. There are usually distinct differences in tone, tempo, volume, or pitch. Try it now—listen (through your memory) and notice the quality of the difference and your response to it. I once met a very quick-speaking New Yorker who felt that many slow speakers were being deliberately rude. Yet he listened to others through a narrow model of professionalism that was known only to his own business group. People may easily evaluate tones, accents, voice speeds, or word choice different from their own as being rude.

When wanting to connect with a person ask yourself, "On what intake channels, (their eyes, their ears, or their feeling senses) does this person seem to focus the most? How does he or she tend to pay attention?" You may want to notice the words they use to describe their inner world. Do they tend to say "I feel," "I view," or "I tell myself"? As you listen, move yourself into their mode, whether this means feeling, hearing, or seeing; and take on a few of their experiential expressions. This allows you to tune in to the world their particular way. You match their valued expressions and the experiential mode of the conversation that they like best. For example, "Do you *see* what I mean, *hear* what I'm saying, or *feel* how this might be useful?"

Deeper Relationships: Shared Interests and Values

When making a deep connection with people, we tend to look for something we have in common. Think of a time you met someone new. The conversation had probably moved in various directions as you looked for commonalities. As a transformational communicator, you can look for skills and interests in common with the person to build a sense of sameness. Rapport may be built through common interests. Does the person have any skills or interests in common with you?

The strongest rapport is created when we respect and understand a person's core values. We become strong listeners when we take time to really pay attention and repeat back the people's value words—the words that describe areas of true importance. On a personal level, you do not need to agree, but for transformational communication, it is important to respect where the other person is coming from. This is an essential part of who your client is. This is noted by the Erickson principle 1, that people are okay just as they are.

CHAPTER 1 Building Rapport to Start Building Relationships

> *Erickson Principle 1:*
> *People are okay just as they are.*

A strong relationship can be formed at the level of shared values. Connection at this level is deep and true. We are all capable of understanding and respecting a person's core values so that we pay attention to him or her as an individual. Be genuinely interested in who a person is, and before you enter into a coaching conversation, be willing to share your own values as well.

Notice that we never know exactly what people mean strictly by the words they say; their meaning and nuance may be slightly (or very) different from our own understanding. However, using their criteria or value words, and even asking them what they specifically mean, shows a deep interest in gaining understanding of their inner world. Practice matching value and criteria words and repeating them back just the way the person has said them, in the same tone and tempo if possible, using them in a slightly different context but with the same emphasis.

Your intention is critical when you use rapport strategies such as matching and pacing. There is a big difference between manipulation and true rapport, and this difference can be felt in the conversation. If your true intention is to build a strong rapport for connection, you will be successful; however, if your intention is to shallowly enter the person's world for a purpose that is not in his or her best interests (such as making money from them without offering value in return), the client will know this at a deeper level and will be turned off by you. The beyond-conscious communication will carry the message "I am not really like you; I am pretending to be like you because I want something from you." Even if rapport is established and these kinds of motives go undetected, an imbalanced relationship will result. Sincerity, integrity, and authentic connection will be lacking and could potentially lead to other, more unfortunate results. Alternatively, if your inner message and authentic intention is "I want to truly understand you, and so I am becoming like you so I can understand," you will be successful in building rapport.

Be aware that people notice, hear, and sense hidden agendas and manipulation. Never use rapport building simply to force a point of view. If you are trying to lead or take a person somewhere in the conversation, be up front and say so. You cannot have a transformational coaching conversation and try to tell, show, or advise at the same time. Telling, showing, and advising violate the coach approach to communication by making the assumption that you know more about a person's life and issues than she does and that she needs to be "fixed."

When you have integrity using a coach approach, the person will see, hear, and feel it, and this makes a powerful difference in the transformative possibility of the conversation. Take time to be congruent with your own authentic values, and take time to move into a coach approach by respecting and understanding your clients for who they are, without judgment or an attempt to change them.

Four Tools for Impactful Communication

When we ask questions that touch "foggy" or sensitive areas, people may have well-built habits to shut down, dissociate, stop communicating, and even get upset. We present four wonderful tools that open the flow of communication, no matter how confrontational a question might be for your client.

Tool One: Verbal Softeners

As we have said, the deepest rapport is built when a person senses that you sincerely care about him or her and you understand and respect where he or she is coming from. A challenging or direct question asked in the middle of such a conversation can break the rapport and the sense of trust that has been established.

For example, imagine being at a party, meeting new people, and enjoying yourself. Suddenly a gentleman you do not know well and have been talking to only for a few minutes asks, "What is your vision for the next year?" What would you respond? How might you feel about this question? Would you share your deepest truth? If you are anything like me, you might wonder why he is asking in the first place. You might think, "Who is this guy? What is his intention? What is he trying to sell me?" You may be on the defensive and not feel you can give an open, honest, and direct answer to such an important aspect of yourself to someone whom you have just met.

When a challenging, provocative, or what might be considered an intrusive question is asked in a conversation, rapport is enhanced and sustained if a verbal softener is used. For example, instead of the gentleman asking point-blank, "What is your vision for the next year?" he might instead say, "You know, I am curious. You seem like such an interesting person, and I am really enjoying our conversation, and I wonder . . . would you mind telling me what your vision is for the next year?"

Notice that all the language before the question was designed to create a relaxed environment that softened the question itself. This way of asking would probably not create a defensive reaction in you. In fact, you might feel like you can share authentically without wondering if there is a hidden agenda or sales pitch behind it.

With any personal or intrusive question, verbal softeners show respect for the person who answers. It is as if we are seeking permission to ask the question. Highly effective communicators, using the coaching approach, employ verbal softeners and pay attention to the results. When softeners are used well, the person usually relaxes and feels that the coach is genuinely interested and is not simply being challenging or manipulative.

The emotional and reticular parts of our brains are quick to sense danger or threat, and that includes being watchful of a person's voice, tone, and word. The use of verbal softeners eases or even removes the sense of threat from any question. When a transformational communicator uses verbal softeners with skill, the person relaxes and there is flow in the conversation.

Here are some examples of softeners.
- Is it okay to ask you what you think about . . . ?
- I appreciate what you are saying and I would love to discover your thoughts about . . .
- May I ask you . . . ?
- I am curious, would you mind sharing . . . ?
- I'd really like to know if you could tell me . . . ?
- Correct me if I'm wrong here, but . . . ?
- I wonder if you will tell me . . . ?
- As you speak to me, I find myself wondering . . . have you noticed that . . . ?
- Are you aware that . . . ?
- It's interesting that you think . . .
- Would you mind telling me . . . ?
- I have a question I would like to ask you; may I?

Tool Two: The Fine Art of Backtracking

Backtracking means feeding back or summarizing information received from a person while managing to find the important nuggets of information. It's the skill of restating key points, using some of the person's own words, matching aspects of the voice tone and body language.

Backtracking builds rapport because the person feels you respect his or her time and clearly want to listen to his or her key message. A person's unconscious use of language tells us exactly what he or she is feeling. When we backtrack with them, using their own words as we restate what they have said, the matching palette of tones and the summary of key ideas shows that they and their feelings have been understood.

Backtracking is similar to paraphrasing or recapping but is not quite the same. People particularly appreciate it if you respond using *their* key value words and show that you understood their main message. People choose certain words to translate their inner world into language. Listen for and use their *exact key words*, those words that had the most emphasis or feeling. If you have not clearly understood the person, he or she will tell you. Continually adjust your response to the response you receive from the person.

If you are confused about the person's points or the direction of the conversation, backtrack the words to regain clarity or ask him or her to backtrack for you. In a conversation it gives you a few minutes to organize your thoughts, notice what has been said, and discover the next important question.

Here are some examples of backtracking phrases:

- So for you . . .
- In other words . . . Is that correct?
- So what you are basically telling me is . . . Am I right here?
- So what you are saying is . . . Do I understand this?
- Let me see if I've got this right . . .
- Now you are clear that . . . Is this right?
  Did I cover all the points?
- Correct me if I'm wrong; you are telling me that . . . ?
- Let's backtrack here . . .

Tool Three: Naming the Outcome in Advance

Deep rapport can be maintained, even with provocative and challenging questions, if you explain why you are asking the question. It's often appropriate, as well as respectful, to tell a client the reason for asking a probing question before you ask it. The person can relax and understand how and why the question is appropriate and supports getting the outcome he or she is seeking, instead of wondering, tensing, or becoming defensive or offensive.

Some examples of how to name the outcome are as follows.

- For the purposes of you really getting what you want from this conversation, may I ask . . . ?

- For the purpose of addressing your immediate concern, would you please tell me . . . ?

- For the purposes of getting to the heart of the issue, may I ask . . . ? So that . . .

- So you can get to the solution very quickly, will you please share . . . ?

- So you can actually make your decision, may I ask . . . ?

Tool Four: Stepping into the Generous Space of Coach Position

The fourth tool, coach position, means mentally stepping out of involvement in the conversation to a Zen detached position where you relax, overview the conversation, and become empty of all charge. In coach position, you view simply from context and let go of getting any result that requires particular content. This rapport tool is by far the most comprehensive and important, and thus has been given a very useful chapter in *Art & Science of Coaching: Process and Flow*.

For now we will look at the power of coach position to set the tone of the warm, relaxed respect needed to begin a real discussion.

As an illustration of coach position, consider the following story.

> *A German canal boatman discovered a boat moving toward him on a long, narrow, one-way stretch of canal where he had been given the right of way and had already traveled several miles. In fury he stomped, yelled, and waved at the approaching boat, which totally blocked his way. Suddenly, he realized that the approaching boat was a derelict. There was not one person on board to hear his swearing.*
>
> *His fury immediately melted, and he found himself completely quiet inside. He was able to follow his own emotional shift, and he started to laugh at his change, noticing the release and how differently he felt in the situation. How can you get angry at an empty boat?*

Coach position means that during a conversation we frequently allow ourselves to move outside of any points of view that require involvement. We are the empty boat. We view and listen to all elements from a neutral observer point of view, from which we simply perceive the conversation as a whole. This makes our conversational partner more comfortable and also more curious about the unique qualities of their own internal conversation. The ability to truly listen necessarily assumes the capacity to step out of any assumptions or narrow conclusions about our conversational partners and their style of thinking or communicating. With a commitment to coach position, we necessarily regain a long-term scope, noticing our partners at discovery points in their lives. Our partners relax as we step into the physical qualities of openness and curiosity.

It is effective to assume Coach Position either by doing it physically with a special posture change, such as taking a deep breath, or through visualizing only, for example, by seeing yourself shifting into observer position in your mind's eye. Some people imagine putting on a special coach position costume, color, or hat. Others imagine viewing the conversation as if from a camera position nearby.

To the extent we keep moving to coach position, we assist our clients in relaxing around their key issues, getting the big picture, and building a systemic view from which they can expand their old viewpoints. Most important, they often match our own relaxation. Physically assuming an overview perspective means that coaches begin to experience the conversation differently as well, often in the way that a symphony conductor relaxes to pace and develop a body of music while the orchestra plays. The coach begins to see the person in new ways and begins to notice current resources that can be made available. The aim is simply to perceive the conversation in a warm way, noticing all the ways that the person is simply okay no matter what his or her own process is. The key is to honor and awaken the genius in the person.

Coach position is an important ingredient in rapport because people begin to get into a meaningful conversation when they feel they can truly relax with you. You do not have an investment in any specific result except to surface the genius within the person, who already has all the resources to be a success.

Erickson Principle 2:
People already have all the resources they need.

In coach position, you step back from the conversation to observe from a resourceful viewpoint of neutral curiosity. This presupposes long-term value, and your conversational partner will relax and start to find it.

In summary, establishing rapport and thereby building trust is the foundation of transformational conversations. There are many other rapport-building capacities we could go into; however, building rapport is about your *intention*.

If your intention is to lead the person somewhere according to your agenda, he or she may feel tense or ill at ease when connecting with you, and a powerful conversation will not be possible. When genuine rapport is missing, real talk with the person will seem difficult, like slogging through quicksand with lead boots.

On the other hand, when your authentic intention is to develop deep rapport with respect, warmth, and openness to support the person according to his or her own agenda, the person will feel at ease. When you support a person in relaxing and trusting deeply, he or she will more naturally move into what is genuinely important and gain more insight and information from the deeper part of his or her own mind.

When communication between two or more individuals reaches its optimum, it might be said that two people are in a *flow state* and of one mind. A state of harmony has been established.

Start everything by developing rapport.

The Rapport Wheel Exercise

We have suggested multiple areas of possible practice in building rapport. Some of these areas may be new ideas for you, some are well-established response habits.

Because rapport happens on multiple levels, a useful personal exercise is to build a rapport wheel (see Figure 1.1) to study your satisfaction with your skills in matching and dancing with many different kinds of people. Simply notice the areas where you easily match people as well as the areas in which it is still a stretch to notice their patterns and comfortably dance with them their way.

In Figure 1.1 we list some of the key rapport areas mentioned so far, placing them on a hypothetical relationship wheel.

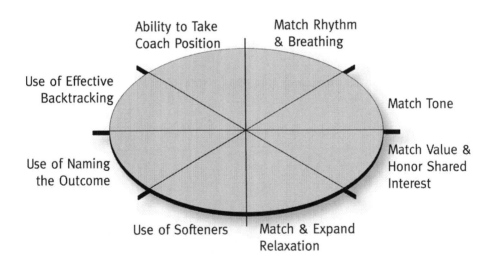

Figure 1.1: Rapport and Relationships

As an exercise you may find it is useful to use this example as a model and build your own eight-part rapport practice wheel. The first step is to select some rapport skills discussed in this chapter and study your current effectiveness by measuring it on your wheel. Evaluate your current level of effectiveness by measuring each rapport skill area on a scale from 1 (needs work, from the center of the circle) to 10 (excellent, at the edge of the circle). Figure 1.2 illustrates an example of a personal wheel.

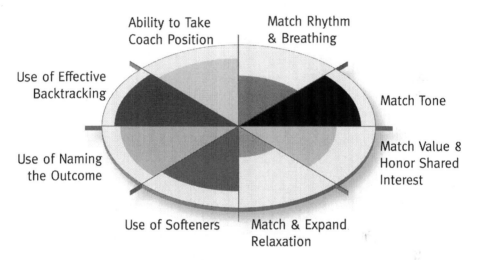

Figure 1.2: Example Rapport Wheel

By looking at the completed wheel, you can quickly notice the areas where you may want to practice and develop stronger personal flexibility.

- Which areas do you suspect could really strengthen your inner dance partner should you commit yourself to a few minutes of practice with others each day for three weeks?
- How quickly do you suspect you could shift your abilities?
- What would it take to strengthen your rapport muscle?

Pick one area to start.

- What are the necessary supports you can give yourself for the accomplishment?
- Will you do it?

CHAPTER 2

The "Sound" of Powerful Listening

Can you listen for commitment when I'm crying out of pain?

Can you listen for commitment when I'm deeply into shame?

Can you listen to my story and still move the veil apart?

Can you notice how I'm hiding and still celebrate my heart?

Can you notice when I'm challenged I might sing the old refrain,

Yet stand firmly for my commitment and call me home again?

—Anonymous

Beyond Automatic Listening

We all have experienced moments in which we have been listened to by someone who cared and experienced the difference that real listening can make. Powerful listening from the heart (as noted in the poem above) is an incredible experience both for the listener and the one being heard.

Yet most of us listen on a very surface or automatic level as we go through the activities of our day-to-day life. We sort what we hear according to what it means for us. We focus on what the people around us are saying, and listen in a self-centered way for how it impacts us.

Take a moment and think of a time when you felt really heard. Remember when someone listened to you and heard what was really important to you on the deepest level. What was this experience like? Did you feel appreciated for who you are? Did you feel trusting of this person and safe to share your truth? Did you feel supported and perhaps more powerful?

Being listened to in such a way can be awe-inspiring. Honing your listening skills is an absolute requirement for transformational conversations. Everything in coaching hinges on listening because what we are listening *for* affects where we are speaking *from* and unfolds how we are *being with* and *for* each other.

Listening Through and For Values

As you set your intention to develop deep connections with people and apply the rapport skills of Chapter 1, you are ready to enter step two, which is powerful listening. In fact, the way you listen determines the relevance of the questions you ask and increases the magnetism of your conversation. Powerful listening and effective questioning are fully intertwined.

Asking great questions that help people move into their own strengths and access their priorities might be called the front piece or the engine of the coaching conversation. *Powerful listening* is the power behind the conversation or the fuel that allows great questions to be revealed.

A person's commitment could be described as the essence of how these habits—his or her inner listening and questioning—connect as a whole to create the person's choices. The current way of making choices may or may not support them in getting what they want. In every conversation we can listen powerfully to discern these inner habits and then move to more inclusive thinking landscapes that shift the person forward into workable solutions.

Listening reveals multiple thinking landscapes—from narrowly personal to widely inclusive. For example, listen to friends taking turns discussing the details of their lives. Clearly, listening to others only in terms of content or issues tends to stimulate reciprocal personal content of one's own. On the other hand, if you listen to people with an appreciation for what is most important to them, their deeper value structures, you can clearly hear their overarching values. Through these you can begin to sense their purpose and inner resources.

As you listen appreciatively, noticing what values are most important to the person, you can move even further by intuitively guessing which great questions will draw out the deeper values and crucial issues. You can help them explore their own core values and aims. And as you become able to effectively listen for the transformational vision that is truly calling them, the conversation develops and even more important questions appear.

Listening in this way provides a mirror to a person's deeper truth, and when a person is heard, reflected, and questioned at this level, life transforms.

Provide an Envelope for Listening

Transformational conversation is both a questioning dance and a listening dance. You assist people when you notice what allows for this specific transformational conversation to develop with them!

For example, you can listen to discover what they need for development now, perhaps inviting open-ended questions about their visions or dreams. You will also need to find in yourself the values that correspond—perhaps warm curiosity, for example. All of this provides an *envelope for listening*, and the conversational possibilities start to fulfill and fill the envelope with inspired dialogue.

When using a coach approach in conversations, we want to listen for and celebrate the specific possibility the person is requesting. We invite a solution or project as a specific emergence, and then we listen for signs of its growing presence. In the garden of the mind, responses are planted by assumptions of their total competence; they are watered with powerful questions and listened to with the sun of warm and focused attention. Under these conditions, appreciative conversational partners grow and thrive, like a beautiful flower. In this environment they emerge with their own dream.

This is the listening landscape. We become curious about how the vision will continue and request more clues. Notice that with this vision quest, ideas immediately emerge. With deep interest, everything continues to develop with renewed zest. We listen for the elements of effective completion, and this occurs wonderfully. The way we listen affects all aspects of what gets said and done.

CHAPTER 2 *The "Sound" of Powerful Listening*

On What Level Do You Tend to Listen?

Levels of listening have been approached by various authors in powerful and meaningful ways. We explore the original definition of several authors, particularly Laura Whitworth, Karen Kimsey-House, Henry Kimsey-House, and Phillip Sandahl in their book *Co-Active Coaching*. These authors have succinctly and clearly defined the process of conscious listening by pointing to three levels.

This book will use the basis of their definition and expand the distinctions of the three levels or ways of listening from a Solution-Focused Coaching perspective. The aim is to demonstrate that *how* we are listening, *what* we are listening for, and *who we are being* as we listen are skills and an awareness that you can truly learn and develop.

Level 1 Listening: Content Listening

In level 1 listening, you listen internally and automatically at the content level. The words being said trigger your own processing associatively. Although you can have deep and powerful conversations at level 1, and there can be a lot of rapport in the conversation, you are present for the speaker specifically as a reflector of your own inner world. You respond automatically according to your own internal processing—meaning you respond according to how *you* think, feel, or understand what is being said.

For example, when you hear the speaker, your mind may relate what is said to the content of a similar experience you had. You will agree or disagree with the speaker to credit, discredit, or add to the speaker's thought when formulating your response.

A valuable analogy is to think of a spotlight. Picture someone speaking with the spotlight on him, sharing what he thinks and feels. Now see the spotlight shift to you so that you share what you think and feel about what he said. The spotlight goes back and forth until the conversation is complete. It is how most of us tend to listen most of the time. This standard listening method is personal, automatic, and reflexive.

As another good example, notice what happens when you are listening to a TV program, such as the news. The spotlight is on the TV, and as you hear the news your mind generates a response. As you listen, you are thinking and making judgments about how you feel or what you think about what is being said.

News Anchor says: "Today is going to be a beautiful sunny day."

You think: "Wow! This is wonderful. I am going to call Louise to play tennis."

Or you think: "Gee, it is nice today when I have to work, and yet it rained all weekend. Just my luck!"

At level 1, we may make positive or negative judgments about the person with whom we are conversing. In some situations, especially long-term relationships, this level includes listening to the other person through preformed judgments about them, including whom you think they are and how you expect them to respond or react to you. We do not really hear the person; we mostly hear the prior opinion we have already made.

Friend says: "I really liked that movie."

You think: "Wow! I knew you had great taste. I knew you would love the director and the cinematography."

Or you think: "That is just like you. This movie was bland. You have terrible taste in movies."

CHAPTER 2 The "Sound" of Powerful Listening

Husband says: "I am going to clean up the yard today."

You think: "Yeah, right! I'll believe it when I see it. You'll probably procrastinate until it's dark out!"

Or you think: "How wonderful. Thank you. I am so appreciative of having a beautiful yard."

Level 1 listening is automatic and guided by the way you think about the world around you and your place in it. For this reason, major miscommunications can happen because listening is more about the listener than about the speaker. Level 1 listening is seldom a level from which transformational conversations and integral change usually emerge.

For example, Larry is listening to Judy, who tells him that she is unhappy in her job. Larry begins to think of what it might mean to Judy to leave her job. He lost his job ten years ago and found it devastating for his family. He leaps to a picture in his mind of Judy in the unemployment line and makes a judgment about this picture. Perhaps she will not be able to pay her bills. Lost in his internal ruminating over his issues and concerns, he does not hear what else Judy has to say and jumps in with, "You'll be sorry if you do this, Judy. You should be happy with the good income you are currently getting."

Level 2 Listening: Context, Structure, and Process Listening

Level 2 listening is very different from that of level 1. This level begins as we listen carefully to the other person according to what is most important, and we engage in focused attentive listening from this value structure.

To refer to the spotlight analogy again, when the speaker is sharing and you are listening with level 2 ears, the spotlight is on the speaker the whole time. When he or she speaks, you do not let your mind automatically trigger its insights, good or bad judgments, or personal responses. You focus warmly on what the speaker is saying. This is the level from which you might listen to your favorite speaker present on your favorite topic or pay attention to a deeply engaging conversation.

Level 2 also means you engage in attentive and focused listening from the value you want to provide that will best serve the person in getting what they want from the conversation. When we listen from level 2, we have a "care-full" focus on the other person and what he or she is saying. Our personal value structure might simply be the inner promise to maintain coach position throughout the conversation and awaken the genius within the person who already has the resources to be a success.

Level 2 listening comes from a place of deep honoring and caring, and in turn tends to produce a profound level of rapport, because the person feels truly heard. When we feel that we have been heard in such a way, we experience that we have been understood, and this produces a sense of deep support and satisfaction.

When you, the listener, turn off your inner dialogue—all your judgments, opinions, and suggestions—and focus on the person and what he or she is wanting, needing, or feeling, transformational conversations and integral change start to become possible.

Listening for Competence
Gives Form to Inner Resources

What are some of the key value structures through which we can listen to people? Milton Erickson's principles provide wonderful listening balance points. You can impact your partners strongly when you listen for their competence in terms of these five principles. As outlined in book 1 of this series, these principles are as follows.

Principle 1	*People are okay as they are.*
Principle 2	*People already have all the resources within them to achieve what they want.*
Principle 3	*People always make the best choice they can at the time.*
Principle 4	*Every behavior has a positive intention.*
Principle 5	*Change is inevitable.*

Figure 2.1: Five Erickson Principles

As you do this you will witness how your listening impacts the inner resources they access in the conversation.

Through these principles, you learn to listen to your conversational partner's vision and values. You develop your own ability to listen for their capacity to trust themselves. You support them when you listen to their capabilities to take charge and move strongly. You particularly impact a client when you listen from the aims they have to complete their project well, noticing the capacities and requirements and detailing a strong plan. You learn to ask the kinds of key questions that support them in reaching for their widest range of vision expression, competence expression, and action expression. When you listen for their full integrity on all levels, you naturally and easily find the questions that support their unfolding integrity.

Transformation is especially possible if you hear the person in terms of the Erickson fundamentals while listening to him or her and noticing inner capacity and resourcefulness. This means that you take a moment to notice that how the person speaking is really okay. When you do this you will also notice the following:

1. You drop all of your preferences, judgments, opinions, and suggestions as to what you think about the situation or what the answers are.

2. You operate as an interested, caring, yet impartial observer whose sole purpose for being in the conversation is to support another person in getting what he or she wants.

3. You declare yourself in coach position, and listen as if the person is whole, complete, and perfect just as they are.

When we listen for and expect a client's competence, we can watch a powerful process start to unfold: What we listen for tends to be heard. What we look for tends to be found. With deep listening, the result is that the conversation more easily becomes a rich conversation. The moment becomes energized. People dive in and speak from the heart. They speak from their competence, and they notice the inner form of their own creative competence growing. They learn to move into their true ranges of competence, responding to both tender support and nose-to-nose challenges. They start finding inner humor and wisdom. Most of all, they learn to balance great questions and great listening within themselves! People leave the conversation experiencing that they were truly heard.

Listening to people as the owners and developers of their own vision allows them to feel supported and trust their vision. You can then assist them to listen to the *voice* of the vision and to connect to the *feeling* of vision inside themselves! They are linking to their capacity to be in touch with their inner resources and connect to their own deep purpose.

Listening to people as the owners and developers of their own vision allows them to feel supported and to trust their vision.

For example, remember Larry listening to Judy, who tells him that she is unhappy in her job. Judy continues to tell him her reasons for being unhappy, and this time Larry is totally focused on what she has to say. As a result, he hears Judy as she expresses her concerns about whether she should stay in this job or leave it. When Judy finishes, Larry is able to feed back to her what she has said. Judy finds further clarity in hearing what she said coming from someone else, and she feels that Larry has indeed heard what she had to say and is deeply interested in her needs, feelings, and desires.

Level 3 Listening: Global, Contextual, and Form Listening

Level 3 listening has been called global or contextual listening because from this level we listen for the formation of a meaningful, congruent, and ecological life. This means that it is possible to develop an understanding of the universal or far-reaching context for anything being said. It is a frame for listening in mythic proportions. In other words, we are generously listening for the entire sweep of whole-life development.

Level 3 listening notices more than just the words; it follows the fine distinctions of tonality, mood, pacing, energy, and emotion behind the words. From coach position we maintain an overview or perspective on the whole conversation, and with global listening we pay attention even more to the person's whole-life development in the conversation.

Global listening naturally encompasses level 2 listening and moves beyond it in scope to frame the unfolding development of the person's life through time. We are listening to the events of the moment as a context for hearing who they are becoming. It provides a framework for the awareness of destiny and design and for welcoming their larger vision.

For example, Larry is listening to Judy, who tells him that she is unhappy in her job. Judy continues to tell him her reasons for being unhappy, and Larry is totally focused on what she has to say. He hears the drop in tone and energy when she speaks of her unhappiness. He notices how her words slow when she expresses concerns about whether she should stay in this job or leave. He hears her voice lift as she mentions finding a new job and the new energy filling her tone. He hears her words slow and the energy drop again when she mentions retraining for a new position. Larry is deeply listening to all the communications she is making. He particularly widens his listening to notice Judy as a person, developing her whole life through this conversation.

When Judy finishes, Larry backtracks her words to clarify what she has said to show her that she has been heard, and also chooses to zero in on what her voice tone and pace told him. He then asks permission to ask her few questions. She says yes, and he asks, "What do you really want, Judy?" He listens and then asks again, "Judy, I am curious, what do you want that is even more important to you?" Through his listening and questioning, Judy begins to realize that the real issue she was unable to articulate in words before this moment. By asking, Larry is able to stimulate further discussion, which will bring out Judy's larger dream. He is listening for what she wants to express but had not yet reached her conscious awareness. Now she is putting it into words.

In this example, Larry has demonstrated listening at level 3, which allowed him to catch what Judy was expressing beyond her conscious awareness—the words inside the words. A transformational conversation has started to take place because Judy has become aware of her beyond-conscious dream. Larry deeply listened and reflected back to her what she said. He then asked permission to ask her some questions, and the questions surfaced extremely valuable information she would not have accessed on her own. The powerful questions took her to her own next level, and the level 3 listening allowed for this powerful communication to take place.

CHAPTER 2 The "Sound" of Powerful Listening

Notice that if Larry had listened to Judy as if she was broken and needed his help, the transformational conversation would not have happened. He listened from a more holistic perspective, having internalized the five Ericksonian principles and listened and reflected back to Judy her tone and aim while asking powerful questions. He came from the empowering assumption that she is already whole, complete, functional, powerful, and able. Because Larry listened consciously at level 3, the deep unconscious communication between them transferred the underlying message effectively—possibly even better than the conscious message.

Had Larry held the assumption or judgment that Judy needed "fixing" and was unable to help herself, his posture, energy, and tone would have passed the message "you are broken" to Judy. Her beyond-conscious mind would have picked up on the message immediately and responded on some level—either rebelling by being defensive or taking on the feeling of brokenness he was projecting. In turn, a transformational conversation simply could not have happened.

When you listen to people as if they are broken or need your help, you send a worry message that tends to reinforce their negative limiting beliefs that are likely the result of their programming from childhood. These old programs tend to show up as fear and narrow the gate to dreams and the beyond-conscious mind so that only the words actually spoken are heard. People then emphasize the correctness of their message and let go of their capacity for multiple levels of deep communication and generous listening.

When you, as a coach, create provocative questions after listening at levels 2 and 3 from a perspective of wholeness and listen to the response in the same way, you encourage deeper reflection. Questions that are birthed from such powerful listening will clarify direction, purpose, values, beliefs, expectations, goals, or the insights behind a statement or situation. This new awareness offers the gift of roots and wings to our clients.

The "Big Ears" Exercise

This exercise takes three different conversations you might have over, say, half a day. Achieve these in one day through phoning three friends or family members.

Suppose you had in your clothing drawer (along with your shirts, socks, and mittens), three sets of ears in three different sizes that you could put on and exchange easily, like earmuffs.

In a playful daydream, take out your ears and look at them for a moment. The first pair is very small, tinier than your normal ears. The second pair is somewhat larger, and the third pair is very large with extra antenna features. Visualize these special ears as you metaphorically perceive them. You might see them as special costume accessories that you enjoy trying on.

As you put them on, each different pair naturally and easily connects you into level 1 (context), level 2 (structure and process), and level 3 (global) listening. Each set is something you might feel like wearing from time to time.

Now, as if these were physical items, first pick out the tiny ears and try them on. This first set is level 1 listening. Phone someone for whom it has been a natural habit to listen to as a friend only. Be curious about their news and respond in your normal and automatic fashion at level 1. After the phone call, write down what you notice about the quality of these ears.

Later, have two other conversations wearing the two other pairs of ears for levels 2 and 3. Consciously assume the qualities described for each state ahead of time by metaphorically putting on the ears before each phone call.

CHAPTER 2 *The "Sound" of Powerful Listening*

Write down what difference you noticed from the call and the conversations as you explored your process listening and your global listening experience.

This exercise is a tool you can use to consciously choose the level from which you are listening. Decide the scope of your listening before each coaching session, select the ears you want to wear that will best serve your client, and go!

CHAPTER 3

Questioning versus Telling: The Advice-Free Zone

People are often taught that it is smart to see through each other. In fact our real intelligence begins with our commitment to see each other through.

—Anonymous

The Russian Radio

When I first started teaching courses in Russia in 1989, just after glasnost, I often found myself in countryside health resorts close to major cities. When I arrived at the hotel and opened the door to my room, I was typically greeted by blaring music from a wall radio, because they did not have TVs in the rooms. Often these resorts and their radios were identical, city to city.

The first thing that I did after setting down my luggage was to hunt for the wall radio and turn it off. Yet I would find only a small device built into the wall with one switch for volume. Even when the volume switch was turned down all the way, a tiny sound could still be heard.

The Russian radio would go off at midnight and start again at 6 a.m. I would be in my morning meditation or quietly awake when the scratchy whisper would suddenly start up. The ups and downs of the tiny sound would remain in the recesses of the room and remind me of the system each day.

Moving Beyond Internal Dialogue Repetition

We all have an inner system, a Russian radio, that greets us every morning with orchestrated internal dialogue. It rises with us in the morning and accompanies us through the day. It plays happy or sad and good or bad—the background music of inner tape recordings. It often echoes in the elevators and down the corridors of our minds with habitual repeating

CHAPTER 3 *Questioning versus Telling: The Advice-Free Zone*

evaluations and commentaries. For many people the "inner Russian radio" is overloaded with managerial mind comments, reminders, judgments, tellings, and even scoldings, which steer us in one direction or another.

Coaching is gaining adherents worldwide because people really want to be inspired and re-inspired despite this internal noise. Habits of negative internal dialogue are hard on us. As with the Russian radio, people listen to old songs on their internal radio that play continuously on themes of cynicism and victimhood. We come from cultures filled with negative laments. Most people have no idea how to turn down their agenda items. They might hear tunes like "I could never get that," "I am not good enough," "There's no way I'll ever be able to do that," or "Who am I kidding?"

The Russian radio is the background music of our inner lives, with older than old message systems commenting on all our life events. When people begin to consider what they really want in life, the Russian radio often blares negative limiting beliefs that are the result of programming from the past. What these old message systems lack are passionate questions and moment-by-moment present-tense observations. The radio blasts *what was* (past tense), not *what is* (the moment now).

Transformational coaching conversations can help people turn down the volume while they rebuild their present-tense listening receivers. People can reset their abilities to regain the joyous open frameworks they remember as their natural home station as a small child.

Once we do this, our lives open up. We truly learn to leave the Russian radio in the far back corners, the old hotel rooms of the mind that we no longer need to occupy.

Questions: The Royal Road to Self-Discovery and Skill Discovery

Consider again how one key to a good life is asking great questions. Great questions might be described as our radio tuner, taking us to clear stations with the maximum relevance to our inner alignment and our own life's purpose. In fact, some people say that questions are the answer because being asked powerful questions moves people beyond entangled loops and old internal commentary—the deadening mind noise—into a place of true empowerment. We can find and listen to our own inner and outer truths.

By coaching, we explore the power of depending on great questions rather than relying on assumptions, judgments, or giving advice. Let us turn this into a coaching principle: Transformational communicators ask open-ended questions rather than tell people what to do. Quite simply, when you tell someone what to do you convey the message:
"I know more than you. You need my help. I am an expert in *your* life."

Transformational communicators ask open-ended questions rather than tell people what to do.

When potential coaches first hear this, they often say, "No, I don't think I know more than my client. I am just giving them useful advice." Think about it for a moment. Is this really true?

Every time you give advice, you assume that the person does not have all the resources within to successfully track their own best choices. Notice that embedded in the message is the assumption that the person would not come up with the best answer alone. Therefore, consciously or unconsciously, you assume that you know more than him or her.

Any subtle or blatant telling, suggesting, or offering of advice controls the flow of thoughts in the conversation and is likely to stop the person

CHAPTER 3 *Questioning versus Telling: The Advice-Free Zone*

from listening to his or her own inner guidance. This may also irritate the client and generate defensiveness, justification, and explanation.

The point of asking strong questions with appreciation and curiosity is to get someone to actually listen to what he says both out loud as well as inwardly and conclude, "I am competent and completely able to think through this for myself." The aim is to assist the person in building a strong inner questioning system, until it becomes their own natural habit for inner and outer leadership.

Put yourself in the position of someone telling you what to do. How do you tend to react to this? When we receive advice from others, we tend to act in one of two ways: find a way to either reject it or comply with it. When we indulge in advice giving as a coach, the result falls exactly along these lines. When people say "No" to you mentally and reject what you say, they also discard any value in your message. If they say "Yes" to you mentally and take action on what you say, they will give you responsibility for their success (credit) or lack of it (blame).

For example, notice that if people take action on your advice and it does not work out, they will probably point their finger at you and not take responsibility for their own choices. "Joan has no clue what she is talking about. I never should have done what she told me to do." If it does work out, they will still point their finger at you and give you responsibility by saying, "Joan is so brilliant. I would have been lost without her advice!"

In contrast, when you ask powerful self-discovery–oriented questions, you assist people in accessing their own inner knowing. They begin to fully trust themselves to find their own best choices. In this way, they take full responsibility for their lives.

The power of asking open-ended questions is so important that Chapter 4 is devoted to it. We begin this process here by examining a variety of types of questions and pointing out several principles, from exploring the nature of Chinese menu questions to scaling questions.

Taking Charge of a Project: The Process of Self-Evaluation

One key to effective coaching is the coach's ability to encourage a person to *self-evaluate* and self-disclose aims, vision, and any difficulties that seem to stand in the way, so that he or she can select his or her own best path. We coach the person to reexamine his or her plan and to notice if he or she is now getting what is wanted. We encourage this vision regarding the best next move.

Although you want to promote self-reflection and self-evaluation, it is important to understand that there are some people who self-evaluate all the time. In fact, they find it difficult to stop. They continually self-check against their standards, moment by moment, to determine if they are going a good job. We call these people *internally referenced*. They think that the continuous self-evaluation of how well they're doing is a requirement for their success. Self-evaluation is the palpable atmosphere of their mind.

There are other people in the world who would prefer to depend on the evaluation of others. They are more likely to ask for help or ask people how well they have done, and they listen carefully to all external evaluations and opinions. They prefer others to set the standards, and they turn these standards into external guides to follow. Then they stop all achievement beyond those standards. They know that they've done a good job from the affirmative commentaries of those whose opinions they respect—those of leaders, bosses, or friends. Their standard might also be set from other sources or statistical comparisons. But it tends to be mostly an external guide.

A sail boat sailing into port with a powerful headwind must tack strongly from one extreme to the other. Most people, in their everyday tasks, fall somewhere in between these two extremes of strong internal reference to strong external reference. In part they self-evaluate, and in

CHAPTER 3 *Questioning versus Telling: The Advice-Free Zone*

part they ask for help. However, a difficult project may provide stressors that knock them all the way to one extreme. The capacity to self-evaluate effectively and know which reference points and directional guides will serve our highest aims is key to keep us on track. This capacity opens the door for coaching.

It is crucial to effective coaching that the client or conversational partner is allowed to self-evaluate or self-judge the various steps necessary for effective performance, rather than the coach assuming this role. In other words, a basic aspect of the coaching approach is that we insist that the client do his or her own evaluation, and we resist all desire for us to put on the evaluator's hat.

The coach's job is to encourage the client's responsibility for effective self-evaluation. This means encouraging a wider vision and a developmental aim. If the client has setbacks, we may point out the opportunity for learning. We foster continuous learning by resisting the desire to impose our own requirements that the client follow only the path we think is best and then judge by our own standards.

An Important Distinction: *How* versus *Why*

What makes a question powerful? First of all, a strong question assists us to go further in exploration. In contrast, any question that takes a person to the famous answer "because" tends to close off the conversation. Why? Because!

Notice the word *because* closes off conversation in the same way now as it did for us as a child. "Can I have some gum?" "No!" "Why?" "Because!" Clearly "why-because" questions and responses narrow choices and the ability to explore alternatives. Why-because takes us to old theories, into the past. The use of the word *why*, as it relates to previous choices, pushes people into a justifying or rationalizing mode as they feel the need to defend themselves or explain a past choice. The implied suggestion is "don't go further."

For example, imagine if I asked you, "Why were you late for our meeting?" How would you respond? If you are like many people, you might rationalize and talk about the heavy traffic, car trouble, how your alarm clock did not go off, how your child spilled milk all over you, and so on. This is because why questions elicit justifications and any decision or outcome can be rationalized, explained, and justified in hindsight.

Notice also that why questions about a situation often imply that a person is "wrong." When a person feels that you are implying this, they get caught up in explaining and defending themselves, and in turn a transformational conversation is not possible.

A better way to get feedback from the past and to use it in making effective shifts for the future is to ask "how" questions. *How* tends to uncover the structure of the situation rather than leading to justification.

Useful questions might be:

- How did this situation develop?
- How can we learn from it and move forward?
- How was the conclusion formed? How can we go beyond it?
- How might we make it work better next time?

When aiming to get feedback on any situation from the past, start your questions with *how*, not *why*!

The Future Focus: The *Why* of Importance

A past-focused why question brings out justifications and recriminations. In contrast, when why questions are used for a future focus, they can be very useful for uncovering the values behind a choice or direction.

CHAPTER 3 *Questioning versus Telling: The Advice-Free Zone*

Consider, for example, this question: "Why is having this result important to you?" This question draws out the value of the result. Asking for more detail or the thought process behind an important choice toward the future is extremely useful for clarity, insight, and inspiration. People get inspiration when they delineate what is important about their vision, reviewing the important details to move toward a bright fulfilling future. This type of questioning demonstrates respect for an individual, giving the expectation that they will be able to find their own answers. This type of empowerment on a regular basis says (without words): "I believe you have the solutions. I believe you have the strength and resources to operate on your own in this world and figure it out. You are okay." From this context, a place of deep honoring and trust, people discover their own answers.

Powerful Questions . . .

- Are based in genuine caring and a sincere desire to learn so the person gets what he or she wants.

- Are clear and concise (i.e., fewer words create a more powerful question) and worded in such a way as to awaken the genius within.

- Are asked with a warm tone and softened with the rapport-building techniques (see Chapter 1) so the person feels honored, cared about, and trusted.

- Support joyful learning by triggering resourcefulness, not defensiveness.

- Are often followed with silence so the person has the opportunity to think through the provocative question. Silence also shows that you are genuinely interested in listening.

- Are designed to move the person toward what they desire, not look backward to explain or justify.

- Support congruency and personal alignment with values.
- Create clarity of purpose and direction.
- Empower and design decisions.
- Look from multiple perspectives to give the person wisdom in seeing the bigger picture, thus illuminating and drawing out how to move forward.
- Assist more comprehensive, systemic thinking.
- Develop focus and clarity, leading toward a state of passionate commitment.

The list of powerful questions could go on. Overall, powerful questions follow an outcome orientation (see Chapter 6) and key directions of effective project development—inspiration, implementation, value integration, and completion /satisfaction (as shared in book 1 of this series). Such questions are powerful because they evoke clarity, intention, value, deeper meaning, realizations, understanding, connection, commitment, and action within the person that allow for clear choices.

Brainstorming without Telling: The Chinese Menu Approach

Have you ever noticed that even in the middle of a powerful conversation, people sometimes hit a wall? What are some strong ways for finding options and new choices when this happens? One Ericksonian approach to supporting people when they are stuck and seem to be unable to come up with more choices is to brainstorm a variety of options with the client by using the Chinese menu approach. This technique offers a list of possible options that could be considered by the person and is used as a preliminary way for the client to open up to further discussion and exploration of potential solutions.

CHAPTER 3 *Questioning versus Telling: The Advice-Free Zone*

Milton Erickson, when working with a client, would often start a list that pointed to many possible alternatives. He would say, "Some people in your situation might make a call; go there in person, or they might send a letter [and so on]. What would be the best approach for you to get what you want from this situation?"

With this approach, the idea is for the person to use this open-ended list, provided on the spot by the coach, to begin to compare options, brainstorm new ones, mix and match, and springboard from one item to an even better idea that is appropriate for them. The Chinese menu approach is not telling someone what to do but pointing to multiple alternative choices from which to select. The coach sets a context of multiple possibilities with the client. The brief brainstorm is just a starting point for clients to continue exploring for their own answers. The coach, of course, is unattached to the outcome or the client's use of the brainstorming. A coach's tone is light and curious. Offering a Chinese menu of options is a technique that stimulates creativity.

Coaching Example

In this example, the outcome for the session is for the client to attract the perfect mate into his life. In the conversation, the coach and client are ten minutes into the session. The client pauses, frowns, and looks puzzled when asked how he might begin the process of finding a new romantic partner.

Client: It has been such a long time. I have no idea where to begin.

Coach: Well, everyone might have a different way to begin something when it has been a long time. Sometimes you can make a fresh start by brainstorming and having fun at it, or by going to the library and finding some ideas there, or the Internet may be of interest, or you may get value from remembering how you met people in the past. . . . What ways might work for you?

Client: [Brightening] Hey I have an idea. It might be useful to join some clubs, like a hiking team or a public speaking club.

Coach: [Taking notes on a pad so the client can see his list of ideas] Hey! It looks like you're getting started here. What else occurs to you?

An Example of Powerful Questions: Scaling to Create Momentum

Scaling questions are a wonderful coaching technology and a solid example of how to create powerful questions. Effective use of scaling questions can increase momentum and clarify your client's vision as he explores a project. Timely movement along a scale can be clearly seen and referenced and supports the achievement of multiple outcomes and detailed plans.

With scaling questions, a coach supports clients in getting clear on where they are right now and where they want to go at any given moment. Scaling is a powerful questioning method that checks in with a client and allows him or her to rate along a continuum where he stands with the conversation and with a project. Using scaling, we learn to "move the marker" on our abilities. Seeing the marker move provides satisfaction that we are making good choices at each stage in the learning journey. Scales can also give us an inner measure on our own development. This supports turning values into competencies.

Types of Scaling Questions

What are some typical scaling questions in coaching? The lead-in phrases are often similar, sometimes like this example.

Imagine a scale from 1 to 10, where 1 is minimum satisfaction with the project and 10 is total satisfaction. Notice where are you right now. What number would you put yourself on at this point?

$$1 \leftarrow \nabla \text{----} \nabla \text{----} \nabla \text{----} \nabla \text{----} \nabla \text{----} \nabla \text{----} \nabla \text{----} \nabla \rightarrow 10$$

With this kind of introduction, we address the topic. There are multiple useful explorations, and some of the most often used are listed shortly. We look at beginnings, middles, and completions. We look at what the current level means in terms of growth so far, what the next point would require, what the optimum changes might be, and how other persons observing us in action would scale all the areas just mentioned. We look at past, present, and future.

Let us explore some examples from A to Z.

Action Steps

- What action steps would it take to move from 5 to 6 on your scale?
- What would _____ [other colleagues, project leaders, team players] suggest you have to do to move from 5 to 6?
- What would you be doing differently when your scale moves from 6 to 7? 7 to 8? Or even to 9? And what else?
- What would your _____ [other colleagues, other team players etc.] notice you are doing differently when you reach 9? How will people around you know that you are at a 9? And how else?

Commitment

- How committed are you to following through with this (on a scale from 1 to 10)?
- How would your _____ [team players, colleagues, project leader, other partners involved] scale your commitment to this result?
- Just suppose for a moment that you are really at commitment level 10: What exactly are you doing differently now?
- How will the people around you know that you are at commitment level 10? How else will they know?

Confidence

- How much chance do you give this project (or other business endeavor) for working out? Scale them comparatively.
- On your own inner scale from 1 to 10, how confident are you that you will move up one step to meet this challenge?
- What can you do now to make your confidence move one step higher?
- What is giving you confidence and hope now that you are really going to reach level 10?
- How will people around you recognize your confidence?

Effectiveness with Results

- Suppose it was the end of three months and you are at level 9; how do you know you are at this level? What do you see, hear, or feel that proves that you are at this point?
- How satisfied are you with these current results? Please show me on a scale from 1 to 10.

CHAPTER 3 *Questioning versus Telling: The Advice-Free Zone*

- How comfortable, from 1 to 10, are you with this level of effectiveness?

- How would your _____ [team players, colleagues, project leader, other partners involved] scale this result?

- What would other key people say are the fundamental things that you are doing now that you should definitely keep doing?

- Where do you place each of these examples on your own scale?

- How would your project be different when you are able to be stable at level 8 in the way that you want? What would you be doing differently then?

Motivation

- In six months, where do you anticipate your level of satisfaction to be (between 1 and 10) with this project?

- How much do you desire to transform this situation? [this communication, this project, this department, business community's point of view, etc.]

- How much do you desire to transform this _____ [project, department, business or business community's situation]?

- What else and who else will be affected by what you are doing when you really do reach this point on your scale? Anyone else?

- How excited are you to take action at level 5? What makes your excitement grow stronger?

- To move one small step up the scale, what might you begin to do? What might you do differently?

- Scale the level of importance you feel with this project.
- Looking back from level 10, what truly motivated you to move toward this point? What skills did you build on that supported you in getting to 10? What were some of the best steps you took that got you to 10?

Satisfaction

- I am curious, what has happened recently to move you even more in the direction you want to go on this scale?
- What happened in your development of this project that went a little bit more in the direction that you now want?
- Where were these examples on the scale of satisfaction?
- What were you doing in the examples that you rated higher on the scale that you were not doing in the examples that were lower? What else?
- What exactly might you begin to do differently when you are at your desired point on the scale? What else?
- After this conversation, what would be the first small sign that you have already started taking the next step to make this happen?
- How happy are you with the result you have achieved so far? Where did it put you on your satisfaction scale?

Notice the variety and the power of these questions to pull out insightful information. Many different types of things can be rated in a coaching conversation.

For more examples (on a scale of 1 to 10 with 1 being the lowest and 10 the highest) consider your projects with the following exercises.

Put Scaling into Practice

Here are some interesting and useful topics for building questions around using some of the scaling structures we've covered. Select three to five of the topics and design at least five questions of different types for each, using some of the frameworks we've presented. We give you one question for each to help you get started.

After writing some practice questions, apply them to one of your own projects and notice the value to you . . . from 1 to 10, of course.

Comfort

How comfortable, from 1 to 10, are you with this approach?

Fulfillment

How fulfilling is this area of a key endeavour for you, from 1 to 10?

Milestones

Where are you now with your development on a scale of 1 to 10? (Potential answer: 3).

What is the difference between being at 3 now and not at 1?

What were the most important milestones needed to get you here?

Priority

How much of a priority is this for you right now? Scale it from 1 to 10.

Risk

How much chance do you give this (communication, challenge, project, business endeavour, etc.) of working out powerfully?

An excellent scaling exercise is to start asking a cluster of these scaling questions around one important project in your life. It might take an hour, or it might take ten minutes. You could do it alone or with a coach.

Practice effectively by focusing on the areas where you want the most clarity. Using a group of the most interesting questions you have just read in this chapter, build a series of ten powerful questions you can use to assist yourself in accomplishing what you have started. Use your questions to finish the project with deep satisfaction.

CHAPTER 3 *Questioning versus Telling: The Advice-Free Zone*

The Dear Abby versus Milton Erickson Exercise

Let us go back to our original focus in this chapter and return to the overall value of listening deeply and letting that process take us to powerful questions, because this is the heart of the coaching approach. Truly listening in the advice-free zone often takes a committed period of practice. It also requires personal awareness.

To highlight the difference between advice and coaching, take a moment to review the following letters. Which of these do you think will produce the best results for Sally?

Dear Abby,	Dear Sally,
I have a problem I need your help with. My husband is spending all his free time and all our extra money on his hobbies and ignoring my needs. I feel very frustrated for his lack of regard for me and my needs. My marriage feels like it is failing. What should I do? Thank you, Sally	You need to develop interests of your own or learn to enjoy your husband's interests with him. The only way your marriage will work is for you to be your own person with your own interests, learning to enjoy your husband for who he is. Good luck, Abby

Dear Milton,	Dear Sally,
I have a problem I need your help with. My husband spends all his free time and all our extra money on his hobbies and ignores my needs.	I wonder if you are feeling frustrated because you desire more connection, or perhaps you are feeling disheartened because you really want both your needs to be met? What is your truth?

Dear Milton,

I have a problem I need your help with. My husband spends all his free time and all our extra money on his hobbies and ignores my needs.

I feel very frustrated for his lack of regard for me and my needs. My marriage feels like it is failing.

What should I do?

Thank you,

Sally

Dear Sally,

I wonder if you are feeling frustrated because you desire more connection, or perhaps you are feeling disheartened because you really want both your needs to be met? What is your truth?

As you consider this, may I ask you a few questions?

- What might be worthwhile for you on an even deeper level?
- As you consider your aims, what would be a best result? What do you really want in this situation?
- What sort of person would you need to become to get what you want with ease?
- What two qualities would this person have?
- How might you naturally and easily take on these qualities?
- What are some first steps you might take to best handle this situation?
- What other alternative solutions might be available for you? What are some other steps here?
- What seems to be the best thing to do first?
- When will you do it?

These questions might be challenging to answer and yet only you know the true path to getting what you want. You have all the answers inside of you.

Best regards,

Milton

CHAPTER 3 *Questioning versus Telling: The Advice-Free Zone*

Which letter do you think would support Sally the most? Sometimes people might appreciate and find it easier to be told what to do, yet this rarely supports sustainable change. In embracing the letter from Milton, Sally will be required to step up and engage her whole mind and heart. Just for the record, no one said coaching was easy for the client. We only said it *works best* for long-term sustainable change.

Are you ready to play the Dear Abby versus Milton Erickson game? You will need to find a partner for practicing this exercise.

This exercise, originally designed by Erickson trainer Richard Hyams, builds a fundamental realization of the meaningfulness of the coaching approach through powerful questions.
Each person takes a role, taking turns.

1. Person A thinks of a challenge.
2. Person B acts as Dear Abby and speaks to Person A's challenge for five minutes. The idea is for Person B to give the best possible advice they can.
   - You should do . . .
   - You can handle the situation by . . .
   - The only way to handle this is . . .
   - I think you should . . .
   - My friend has this same challenge and she did . . . Would this work for you?.
3. After five minutes, Person A shares the same challenge and Person B acts as Milton Erickson by listening to Person A as already having the resources to be a success. Then, Person B asks open-ended coaching questions for five minutes, such as these:
   - What are some results that you really want from this situation?

- Why are these results important to you?
- What do you notice when you scale their importance to you from 1 to 10?
- How might you begin to achieve what you want?
- How *else* might you achieve the result you want?

It might be valuable to engage the Chinese menu approach if the client gets stuck. Just be certain the tone is warm brainstorming without attachment to the direction the person takes.

4   After you, as Person B, ask questions for five minutes, stop and invite Person A to share their experience of talking with Dear Abby. Comparatively, ask them their experience of talking with Milton Erickson. Even though you both may know the difference from the outside, it is sometimes surprisingly meaningful to actually do it and to discuss the experience. How does your partner perceive the difference between the approaches?

5   If you have time, have your partner switch roles with you. What did *you* notice?

There are a lot of practical tools in this chapter. Some people may jump in and practice them quickly, some may taste a few and then return to old habits, and some may use the chapter as a reference and gradually practice and apply the different approaches. Some may even find a different way to explore and integrate the coach approach to powerful questions.

We invite you to find your own best way for integrating the most useful of these techniques to asking powerful questions. Your client's inner wisdom is like a treasure chest, full of jewels. As you learn to use the questions here and in the next few chapters, you will be helping them find their own inner wisdom.

CHAPTER 4

Turning on the Tap: The Magic of Open-Ended Questions

Intelligence is not intellect. It is an unfathomable matrix of truth.

—Joseph Chilton Pierce

Einstein on the Porch

A reporter from a scientific journal called and requested an interview with Albert Einstein for a special article on "Great Questions that Great Scientists Ask." Einstein agreed, and the reporter arrived at his home in the last moments of daylight. He discovered Einstein seated in a rocking chair on his porch, puffing on a well-worn pipe and watching the sunset.

"I have only one question to ask you, Dr. Einstein," said the reporter, a bright and nervous young man with a notebook. "This is the key question we are asking every scientist we can find. The question is: 'What is the most important question that a scientist can ask?'"

Einstein sat in his rocking chair with his eyes twinkling. The elderly scientist stretched back and thought for ten minutes. "That is a great question young man, and it deserves a serious answer," he said. With that he commenced to rocking slowly on his chair and puffing on his pipe. He remained silent, deep in thought for another few minutes, while the reporter waited expectantly for some significant mathematical formula or quantum hypothesis.

The question that the reporter received instead has had the world thinking carefully ever since. "Young man," Einstein said gravely, "the most important question that any person can ask is whether or not the universe is a friendly place."

What do you mean?" answered the reporter. "How can that be the most important question?"

Einstein responded solemnly, "Because the answer we find determines what we do with our lives. If the universe is a friendly place, we will spend our time building bridges. Otherwise people use all their time to build walls. We decide."

CHAPTER 4 *Turning on the Tap: The Magic of Open-Ended Questions*

This story illustrates Albert Einstein's approach to great questions late in his life. We see the power of open-ended questions in this example. His approach shows how a powerful question can move people past old thinking habits and into spacious mind-heart connections, linking values and vision.

The Nature of Great Questions

We immediately notice our inner response when someone asks us a great question—the endorphins rush, the ideas flash, and we become curious and start to think on a new level. The question takes us on a search, and the search leads us into unique and useful territory. We all have this ability to stretch the mind, to truly ponder what is deeply significant to us.

Most questions do not do this. In the last chapter we noticed some reasons behind this: the person with a question might have an agenda to teach us, evaluate us, or direct us. The questions might lead us into the past, where we are asked to explain, justify, or rationalize our choices, thoughts, and outcomes. Such questions often lead us into a tailspin. Or it may be a simplistic why-because question and take us into the past or into specific details that require action now, such as, "Will you pass the salt?"

Great questions have a consistent *structure* that you can learn to use again and again. People writing books on great questions will give you lists of questions, and of course, in this book we will do so, too. But listing great questions is just sharing tips that may or may not be useful considering the multiple unique contexts of coaching conversations.

This book is designed to do something much more useful for you than just offer engaging lists of questions. Our aim is to train you in powerful question-building strategies through open listening and open-ended questions, finding questions that truly support the client's outcomes. *Open-ended* is also an attitude. We can have open-ended approaches to visualization and discovery processes. Loosely speaking, we can have open-ended, appreciative voice tones. Understanding the idea of being open-ended adds to the power of the open-ended solution-focused approach.

> *Being open-ended adds to the power*
> *of the solution-focused approach.*

The nature of great questions—questions that start a true flow of inquiry—is recognizing that they have a design that engages us and starts us pondering. We find our own answers around our own life content. This helps us structure our inner knowing so that we add personal meaning and knowledge to our lives and move toward day-by-day living from our own real values. Great questions guide us toward determining our deepest purpose and strongest future.

The Power of Open-Ended Questions

In continuing the exploration of powerful questions, it is important to explore the structure of strong open-ended questions. It is especially useful to learn how to open up any question so that it stimulates a flow of ideas. This is like turning on a tap. We can ask trickling questions or we can ask geyser questions that have a huge impact.

Open-ended questioning of the geyser variety is the topic of this chapter. The power of open-ended questions is that they create flow state

CHAPTER 4 *Turning on the Tap: The Magic of Open-Ended Questions*

awareness in multiple ways by continuously and purposely noticing what approaches open things up. In other words, everyone can systematically discern the difference between questions that move an exploration forward energetically and those that do not. There is a science to value-vision connection. Solution-focused coaching means discovering how to open the floodgates of the motivated mind.

Practicing the exercises in this chapter will teach coaching effectiveness quickly. With even three weeks of strong practice, you can become an artist in open-ended questions. As you will see, it soon becomes possible to subjectively scale the level of impact of any question that you ask.

Open-Ended versus Closed Questions

Recall from the last chapter that giving advice often comes from the belief that the person is not whole, not capable, and does not have the needed resources to figure out their next choice. "Telling" is commonly used to straighten someone out about something and does not acknowledge the Ericksonian principles that people are perfectly okay. This does not serve a person well through time.

Open-ended questioning, on the other hand, stimulates inquisitiveness, resourcefulness, and deep thinking. It opens the door to inner learning. Most important, effective open-ended questioning gives a person the opportunity to move past old gremlins or fears (especially the fear of dreaming), as well as any limiting theories about life or themselves. It allows people to come up with their own integral insights and solutions that make sense. This approach serves a person well through time.

A closed question requires only a yes/no or this/that answer and tends to dead-end the conversation. Open-ended questions encourage the person's deeper reflection. People tend to respond freely and openly because open-ended questions require a different level of thinking than a yes/no or either/or answer.

Open-ended questions invite people to relax, look deeply into themselves, listen to themselves, and get clear on their *own* perspectives. Open-ended questions lead the client away from the limiting loops of either/or thinking, judgment, and limitations, so that the person begins sharing his or her deeper thinking and discovers creative ideas that ignite learning and inspiration.

Open-ended questions often warm the heart. They evoke an inspired mental state of discovery, insight, commitment, and action, rather than focus on the challenges of the past. When used with a future focus, open-ended questions move people into a fresh vision as they trigger powerful images of what they want.

For a coach, open-ended questioning demonstrates respect for a person because it holds an expectation that they will be able to find their own answers. This type of empowerment implies that the client has the solutions and the strength and resources to operate on his or her own in this world and figure it out. From this context, a place of deep honoring and trust, people *do* discover their own answers.

The Tone of Open-Ended Questions

A powerful open-ended question is generally phrased gently, in a way that invites the client to go within and return with a thoughtful response. If a powerful question is not phrased gently and in an open-ended, curious tone, it can be viewed as criticism or manipulation that may create a defensive reaction, which in turn negates the quality of the question.

Tone is part of the communication message, and it is extremely important, especially when asking a question that gets to the heart of the matter. A softened and supportive tone minimizes the possibilities of triggering a defensive reaction. The overall message received by the person's beyond-conscious mind must be, "This person cares and really wants me to engage with this. She is holding my agenda and I trust her."

CHAPTER 4 *Turning on the Tap: The Magic of Open-Ended Questions*

Opening Out: Discovering Choices

When penetrating, non evaluative, outcome-oriented questions are formed, the unspoken or unrealized compelling issues start to become clearer. In turn, people move beyond their habitual structures of thinking and consider their situation more deeply and in a different light. In doing so, they discover their own inner magnet of motivational visions, values, and choices.

When solutions and actions are coming entirely from the client's own mind and intention, he or she will learn to take 100 percent responsibility for his of her actions and thinking. The ownership of a solution is not in question if it has been primarily produced by the client.

This assists people in breaking the old habit of seeking advice and getting someone else to tell them what to do. When a person is not given the opportunity to come up with his or her own answers, he or she does not take ownership, and without ownership the person will not take full responsibility for the results—whether the outcome is positive or less than life enhancing.

In summary, use open-ended questions when you want to accomplish the following.

- Elicit ideas, input, and recommendations that create a higher level of personal investment, involvement, accountability, and responsibility.
- Help people understand the roles they played in their past results and help them achieve improved results.
- Train people to contemplate their thinking processes, the old theories, the direction, and the conclusions they have created.
- Change the focus of the conversation from a past-centered focus to a future-centered focus (with careful wording). The

choice of wording can also be used to focus attention on discovering solutions, possibilities, and creative inspiration instead of staying stuck.

Making Open-Ended Questions Even More Open-Ended

Designing powerful open-ended questions is an art. An easy way to learn is to practice sensing interest levels in the question. If you build a scale from 1 (slightly open-ended) to 10 (fully open as far as we can go), you can see how to turn on the tap of inner interest from a trickle to a flood. See Figure 4.1 for an illustration of creating open-ended questions that lead to transformational change

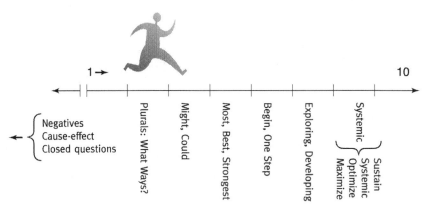

Figure 4.1: The Open-Ended Line

CHAPTER 4 *Turning on the Tap: The Magic of Open-Ended Questions*

Here is a list of how a simple question can move on this continuum of becoming more open-ended.

- **Negative**: Why don't I have enough time?
- **Closed**: Is there a way I can create more time?
- **Open**: How can I create more time for myself?
- **More Open-Ended**: What are some of the ways I could create more time for myself?
- **Focused**: What might be some of the *best* ways?
- **System Thinking**: What are some of the ways I can maximize time use, every day of my life?

Various additions will increase the interest level in your question. Finding a fresh question that slightly widens the value base of the client evokes his or her deeper interest. The person starts pondering the best alternatives or stronger choices.

Explore this around an issue of your own by asking yourself these questions.

1. One way to open and widen interest in a potential choice is to use the words might or could. For example, you could change the question, "How will you go deeper into your exploration?" to "How might you go deeper into your exploration?"

   Other examples:

   - How *might* you learn even more?
   - How *could* you find even more value in this task?
   - Who *might* you ask to support you?

67

2. Another method is to make your question plural. Notice that several results widen interest beyond one result.

- What are *some ways* you might learn from doing this?

- What are *some* useful results you want from this situation?

- What are *some other ways* you will find value from this choice for the long term?

Play for a moment with the examples of open-ended questions below, and use either the words *could* or *might* or simple plurals to make them more open-ended. Try them around your own issue/project. See if they encourage deeper reflection. Does shifting the language move the scale of interest so that you strengthen your interest in your results?

- What will you learn from doing this?

- What is it you want from this situation?

- How will your ability grow by taking on this task?

- What will inspire you in doing the task?

3. Adding words like *great* or *best* or *most important* can bring more power and focus to an open-ended question. Notice, with the foregoing examples, we can turn on the flow tap further to make them even more open-ended and powerful. For example,

- What are a few of the *best* things you can learn from doing this?

CHAPTER 4 *Turning on the Tap: The Magic of Open-Ended Questions*

- What are some of the *most important* things you might want from this situation?

- What are some of the *best* ways to be committed for the long term?

4   Explore widening the scope of verbs. Begin to explore the power of using open-ended verbs, especially using the continuous flow that starts with adding -ing to create *moving* examples. Moving is always more open ended that anything static. Try words like these:

- developing
- inspiring
- growing
- evolving
- learning
- clarifying
- creating

Example questions might be as follows.

- What are some of the best ways for *discovering* your power with this?

- How might you start *learning* even more about these questioning methods?

- What good ways for *enjoying* this process come to mind?

Create a few more sentences using sample verbs from the list and others that occur to you and put them in an open-ended format. Be certain to keep the questions clear and with a laser focus. Adding a lot of unnecessary words can get in the way of effective communication.

5   Now you can bring in *system thinking*. This is thinking about the nature of a workable whole system, not just examining one subsystem. System-oriented approaches increase your effectiveness with open-ended skill sets and strengthen the power of your reach.

We want to stimulate a view of a whole system, and appropriate questions are designed to trigger visual images like a match to dry kindling. It can be any kind of whole system that is relevant to the client's outcome for the conversation. For example your lifetime is a whole system, and so are your body, your family, neighborhood, city, and country. A musical scale is a whole system, as is a geometric form like a circle or a square. A numbering scale, say, from 1 to 10, is a whole system. What other whole systems come to mind? Can you create some by declaration?

You can use a maximum value question to enhance any approaches toward your system of choice. If the question is designed to create movement toward the optimum result or maximum value of using that system, you will excite a compelling interest in exploring the idea. By using words that maximize (*best, great, finest*), you can add wind to your open-ended system sails to sail powerfully towards the system of choice.

For example, consider the following:

- What could be your best result if you scale some alternatives from 1 to 10?

- Suppose you could read your whole life story in a book and really explore your life through every chapter. What are some great ways you could use this book to maximize your understanding of your whole life purpose? How could you start developing some small part of this understanding even today?

CHAPTER 4 *Turning on the Tap: The Magic of Open-Ended Questions*

- What if you woke up tomorrow morning to discover that in the night a magical wind had come up and blown through everything, getting rid of all the negative things in your life? All your old cynicisms about yourself and some areas of your life have been completely whisked away. Suddenly you find it possible to optimize your natural inner skill in the art of real happiness. What are some of the great ways you can begin to adapt this into your life?

The Open-Ended Line Exercise

To explore open-ended thinking and questioning, you can practice by putting a two to four-meter line on your floor, perhaps from one wall to another, using simple markers or tape. Let one end equal 1 on a 1 to 10 scale. The other end, then, is 10.

Think of one of your key projects and ask yourself a question about getting results. Notice the degree of open or closed in the very first formulation of your question that you use. This observation gradually trains you in the open-ended reach that is used by solution-focused coaches. (You will learn how to pace and lead individual clients to their own level of open-ended thinking.)

Let's go through an example step by step. Suppose you notice a regular thought process that causes you dismay. For example, you sometimes voice internally to yourself a closed, negative question with a giant generalization: Why don't I make any real money?

1 If this thought started your project question, you might put this particular question as only a 1 out of 10 in your open-ended formulation. (Note that any question starts us at least at a 1 on the scale, because it will be more open than any statement or conclusion

where there is no measure at all. To say, "I can't make any real money" snaps the mind shut, and you become only a visitor in your thoughts.)

Notice that this provocative question is a negative why-because complaint. By design it automatically has the questioner generate reasons (possibly excuses) why not. For many people, such a question provokes internal dialogue with their inner critic answering any ideas that emerge with challenges: "Because you really don't seem to have the talent, or because you don't make the right efforts, or because you're so darn stupid!"

Now take a second step up the open-ended line using this money-making example and explore how to make the theme question more useful.

What might the next step be?

2   Review this revised question:
    "Why am I always struggling to make ends meet?"

You have moved to a positive formulation to turn on a tiny bit of curiosity, though it is a why-because question and still tends to focus on one cause and on the past. Again, you mentally go for the reasons that compile negative theories you have already built.

3   Follow the money-making example and move up the line. Now one might say, "How can I make more money?"

Here we formulate a basic open-ended question. Notice that this genuinely curious question helps the asker view possibilities and immediately begins to allow you to begin thinking in a truly open-ended

CHAPTER 4 *Turning on the Tap: The Magic of Open-Ended Questions*

way. The open-ended flow tap has been turned on, and a small flow begins, although negative conclusions and fear formulations might still appear at any time.

4   Now, how might the previous step lead to another level of open-endedness? Think of some of the example sentences we worked with before, and begin to add in some open-ended boosters, such as *beginning* or *starting*. Beginning anything is always the most open-ended point for people. For example, "What are some ways I could *begin* to make more money?"

What might be some of your other amplification ideas?

5   How might you create a robust move from the previous step? If you recall, you can add in maximum value words like *great*, *most important*, and *best way*. These curiosity boosters grab attention and take us into internal formulations where we overview choices and select the strongest response. For example: "What is one *great* way I could start to earn money?"

6   Now explore the power of plurals:

"What are some of the best ways I could start to earn money?" Or even, "What are three great ways I could start to earn more money?"

7   Now move even further and add in a systems approach. For example, we can move to a question like this: "What are some great systems I could use to begin to maximize my earning power quickly?"

8. At this point we open the door to using the systems developed to expand all systemic frameworks available. This means we shift to the power of multiples and try on various systems of points of view. We might also build some frameworks to cover our multiple alternative points of view. Consider the following example.

"Here I am and it is one year from today [name the day and year], and I have taken complete control of my earning power, leveraging my abilities in some strategic ways and really developing a system for producing results.

- What were some of the choices I considered?
- What were some of the very best ways (say, ten of them)?
- What were the three ways that were the best of the best and got me to where I am now?
- Standing in this future point, looking through the eyes of my colleague, friends, family, what qualities do I notice about the self that they now see?
- When I look back from this future point, what are some of the landmark learnings and risk taking I see?
- As I float way up and see all of time—the moments from now to this future point where I have achieved my outcome—what are the best ways I see myself maximizing my opportunities and building my earning power?
- What actions will I take now that go even further, so I am clear on the future I am moving into?

Do this exercise with two of your most persistent internal complaints—for example, money, certain relationships, building a business, renewing a healthy lifestyle, developing coaching skills, and so forth.

CHAPTER 4 *Turning on the Tap: The Magic of Open-Ended Questions*

If you can do this with yourself, you will learn how to think as an open-ended specialist and will quickly begin to make a huge difference in the lives of others. As you continue, you will grow to develop mastery as a coach.

For this exercise we only invite you to move to 7 or 8 on your own line of formerly closed ideas and just wonder about the end of the line. We will show you some powerful ways to launch to the next level of great open-ended methods. There are several reasons to take your time with this both for yourself and your clients: You are actually building nervous system highways as you open your attention with powerful questions. You are developing inner systems to create the mind/brain flexibility that these questions require.

With continued practice, you learn to reach further into the depths of your own creativity, and your pondering power becomes enhanced. The same is also true for your clients and teams. Assist them in building their pondering power, moving step by step and stopping naturally when the task is achieved. Just be curious and move with the flow of the topic, only asking your questions one step ahead at a time, and notice how this works for them.

Powerful Questions from Coach Position

As we've discussed, asking open-ended questions creates trust in a conversation. It supports people in having the opportunity to generate their own insights and solutions. When you ask the most open-ended question in the moment that moves the client toward his or her outcome, you will be doing highly effective coaching that can immediately get to the heart of the matter to support people in starting to think through their deeper aims.

When open-ended questions are used effectively in any dialogue, they draw a deeper realization from the person, which can effectively illuminate the situation in a new way. Open-ended questions are authentic and thoughtful and come from a sincere interest to know more about the person's insights or solutions. Open questions are clean, implying that nothing is in the way of the question landing powerfully for the person. Less is more when asking powerful questions—sticking to a single issue, addressing only one challenge at a time, and using the least number of words possible allow the questions to be clean and effective.

Typically, open-ended questions, due to their power and simplicity, are often followed by a long pause or a respectful silence. As a transformational communicator, you will learn to be comfortable with this silence because it allows the person to ask themselves what is most important and listen inwardly for his or her own answers. It demonstrates your caring and your sincere interest and commitment to listening deeply.

As you open up your mind and heart from coach position and ask questions that open the client's mind and heart, bigger and better possibilities will arise that support the client in being, doing, and having more in life. At the same time, you are learning these coaching approaches to maximize value for yourself. The exciting thing about coaching is that when you hold the open-ended space for another, you indirectly receive in ways you never dreamed possible. This immediately becomes available through the power of your open-ended questions.

CHAPTER 5

The Secret Tones of Transformation

There is a self reality . . . Your real self. Its nature is timeless awareness. . . . It never ceases to experience infinite expression. It is unwavering. It is Spirit itself.

—Shankara

The Story of Tommy the Hermit

There I was among tall Saguaro cacti, big boulders, craggy mountain peaks, and a winding trail going over hill and dale from open areas into deep canyons. I spent three days in some of the most isolated yet astounding wilderness in North America, the Superstition Mountains of rural Nevada, with a small backpack, a large water skin, and a well-thumbed map. I had not seen another person for two days. It was time to find a camp for my third night in the open, and I turned off on a small meandering trail toward a tree-filled area half a mile away at the base of a rugged cliff front beside the mountain.

As I entered the area, I was amazed to see large white round stones lined up on each side of the path. I moved through a canopy of branches to walk into a well-organized open camp with several tents and fire pits. I was in someone's home.

A very small man with big eyes, a warm smile, and a gray beard came toward me. He was dwarf-sized and looked up at me through shaggy locks of gray hair. He extended his hand. "Tommy's the name!" Somewhat shocked by his presence, let alone his size and appearance, I introduced myself as if this was an expected occasion. He chose to treat my appearance as a happy surprise. "You're my first visitor in ten years," he announced. "Would you have dinner with me?"

Two rather surprised people sitting by the fire in the deep wilderness, eating beans and drinking coffee and glad to see each other was an astonishing happening. I relaxed and listened to Tommy's stories. He talked about fifteen years of hunting for the Lost Dutchman Gold Mine. ("See all those holes in the mountain over there?") He was proud of his achievements. ("Didn't find the Lost Dutchman Mine yet, but I'm going to. This is the right spot to dig!")

He was talkative. He didn't ask me much about myself, but shared story after story. He showed me the verses of the Bible he was currently copying by hand in large, half-inch script for his mother in Louisiana, who was nearly blind.

"She depends on me to send her Bible verses she can read," he said. "And she is funding my expedition. She sends me a check every two months, and I go out for grub and mail her some verses. When I find the gold, she is going to have a happy retirement."

His comments puzzled me, but I accepted them. His task and his role to himself seemed totally legitimate. His solitary life had a real function. I thought to myself, "Everyone has their own special place in the world. Well, now I get to meet a really strange one!"

So now I knew his plot. Shortly, he knew mine: touring the wild country for a short "get to know myself, get to know the land, and get to know real silence" vigil. That puzzled him, but he accepted it. Obviously I was a strange one to him.

Picture the scene: Two strange ones talking together, pleased for a chance to celebrate simply being human. Each is being courteous about the other's strangeness. They sit on a star-spangled night in the middle of the wilderness—one campfire, two humans, a pot of beans. Each listens to the other from a model of the world that comes from totally different realities.

There was not a lot to say, but we found a way to say it. He told me about the birds, the insects, and the lizards. I listened and asked questions about the tame pigeons that cooed softly as they roosted above his head. "My friends," he said.

I expressed enthusiasm for the mountains, and he radiated pleasure. I listened as he spoke with pride about the birds and his home in the wilderness. I respected his energy and his resourcefulness. Neighbors can be neighborly anywhere.

I told him of some of my own fears from several nights when wild coyotes could be heard in the underbrush. He expressed assurance that I would be safe on the return journey. I relaxed listening to his travel tips and hearing his friendly tone.

We talked about the amazing array of stars visible from the high country. "Yup!" he said, "God is sure present out here." I nodded. Together we noticed the wholeness and shared the experience of beauty and blessing.

I turned into my sleeping bag, assured of safety and friendship from an odd stranger. He turned into his own quarters having been visited by a real friend. I no longer thought of him as a hermit, but as a member of the mighty family of my friends. I began to envision a worldwide clan of friends, persons who help each other rebuild their faith in themselves by offering basic human assistance and warmth when needed, no matter how strange the encounter.

I headed back the next morning, never to return. Tommy remains in my thoughts to this day. The experience gave me a perspective on the nature of human friendship I had never considered before. There is no such thing as a hermit, and nobody lives alone. Humanity allows no corner to hide in. We must love one another or die.

Using Your Coaching Voice for Maximum Impact

Open-ended vocal tonality is very powerful and necessary in a transformational conversation. What makes a vocal tone open-ended is the extent to which it radiates sincerity and relaxed interest. You would have heard such a tone if you listened in on the conversation with Tommy.

With an open tone, we hear a respectful quality of appreciation. Appreciation, after all, is like interest. *Interest*, in all meanings of the word, appreciates—it endlessly adds to itself. In other words, to appreciate means to grow more of. We can speak and listen from open-ended appreciation, and this creates a feeling tone in a conversation that supports insight, awakened possibility, and transformation.

Cultivating a Range of Tones

There are three powerful vocal tones—tone of the wizard, tone of the true friend, and tone of the visionary elder—that open the doorway to one's deeper knowing mind and also sharpen the capacity to appreciate the inner values and capabilities of others. They are the qualities of voice and modulation. These tonal nuances are immediately understandable in multiple languages.

These tones use the power of up-tempo sound and warmth so that the client gets an uplifting experience from the voice itself. Almost always a boost is experienced with an open-ended question expressed in an open tone.

Let us try these powerful tones. You will want to use them on a regular basis because these tones move you and those with whom you converse beyond the grasp of either/or simplifying frameworks of thought. Most important, they will also move people beyond cynical, judgmental internal dialogue that assertively pigeonholes labels and creates bad feelings. Through your tone alone, people can develop easy access to thoughtful values and vision flow states when connecting with you.

Open-Ended Tone 1: The Tone of the Wizard

The tone of the wizard is an important coaching tone. The voice is upbeat, up-tempo, engaged, and value-based, all at the same time. It is robust and enthusiastic. There is both an expectation and a request for competence. The wizard tone goes with questions that trigger and encourage enthusiastic visualization. The voice generates appreciation of possibilities and opens future engagement. It orients to questions about strategies and resources.

The Request Function: The Tone of the Wizard

- Upbeat, strategic, and open!
  Requests competence.

- Shows enthusiasm and energy.
  The voice tone is curious with lots of questions.

- You have resources; let's get a strategy here . .

Practice Phrases

Use these phrases to practice expressing both the phrasing and tone of the wizard. Speak aloud, listening to your voice quality. Imagine that you are talking to a coaching client, and the aim is raising the energy around a strong plan. Your voice nearly whistles with enthusiastic questions. Try short, enthusiastic questions for energy. You might rub your hands in glee to get yourself into the frame of mind.

CHAPTER 5 *The Secret Tones of Transformation*

- You are really sounding focused now! As you see that moving along so well for you, where do you go next with this?
- Hey, now you're getting some ideas! What else?
- What strategy might you develop to do this well?
- Look out! You're really on a roll now!
- Hey, you're getting me excited here! Keep describing your big picture, and I'll look at it with you!
- Nobody ever told me what you're like when you get fired up! You're really sizzling now! Tell me more!
- Now there's a scenario worth considering! Keep going, unfold it even more; this is interesting!
- Did anyone ever tell you how creative you are when you look at the big picture?
- Hey, your enthusiasm is on the rise. Watch out!
- Listening to you now, I know that you're a true learner. Way to go!
- You're such a visionary! Just keep dazzling me with the details in this picture! Tell me more.
- Imagine that! . . . What else could you see yourself doing to make this happen?

Open-Ended Tone 2: The Tone of the True Friend

The second tone, the tone of the true friend, woos a person toward self-appreciation in the face of difficulty. It is designed to generate self-forgiveness for old mistakes and provide unconditional support. The voice is warm and open, light, and particularly tender.

> ### The Promise Function: The Tone of the True Friend
>
> - Woos one toward appreciation and generous forgiveness.
>
> - Associative and warm, open, and promise of ability.
>
> - Softness, tenderness in voice.

Practice Phrases

Use these phrases to practice using the tone of the true friend. Slow your word pacing down a bit. Imagine your voice having some of the qualities of a gentle, encouraging mother.

- You and the rest of the world just might get a little bit discouraged with that one!

- Are you going to move past this? You deserve to give yourself a little support here.

- Would you mind? Just set the emotion aside for a moment and widen your vision. How might your future, wiser self support you to learn from this difficult moment?

- You've got to be kidding! You really blamed yourself for this? Knocking yourself can hurt a bit, doesn't it? How can you use it to move further?

- Would you just take a moment and dial up that part of your self that speaks in that self-derogatory way and have it just listen for a moment to the part of yourself that doesn't take that kind of nonsense, the part that knows that you are truly okay and always have been?

- That is an important inner connection, isn't it? What does that supportive part of you say in the face of these fears?

- No wonder you felt down! Knocking yourself gets to anyone! Thanks for sharing what that was all about for you. Now, step *way* out. How might you let go of this?
- Wow! Who *wouldn't* feel that way believing that? I'm so glad you are now talking about it.
- Take a deep breath. In a moment you will loosen up, and you will get your vision back.
- Is it possible you are being a tad unkind to yourself in this situation? Is it possible that you deserve a bit of a break here?
- Is it possible that you have been both judge and jury on yourself and haven't been fair to yourself at all?
- What if, in fact, you're really okay? What if you're just a bit discouraged?

Open-Ended Tone 3: The Tone of the Visionary Elder

The tone of the visionary elder is like a full-bodied bell gently ringing in new possibilities, and sounding clearly with the highest resonant tone in the available range. The vocal tone shows leadership in quiet thanksgiving and celebration. If it were music, the resonance would be like Beethoven's *Ode to Joy*. The focus is on championing inner resources. There is a quiet note of transformational blessing. There is the experience of benediction, ongoing development, unfolding power, and purpose. This tone usually comes into play toward the end of a coaching session.

> ## The Declaration Function: The Tone of the Visionary Elder
>
> - The declaration of blessing, benediction, and ongoing development.
>
> - Openness, spaciousness in vocalization:
>   "You are whole and complete."

Practice Phrases

Use these phrases to practice your skills with the tone of the visionary elder. Once you get a sense of its expansive inner space of benediction, add even more range into your speaking. Imagine yourself revitalizing life through this warm, expansive voice that rolls out softly like an ocean and expresses the voice of the world in celebration. Speak in a relaxed way, hearing the wisdom in your words. Try the tone now.

- Only *you* know your own inner truth and why this is meaningful to you. Only *you* can step into your power now.

- You are really learning! Your groundswell of abilities is on the rise. Your capabilities will carry you a long way.

- As you talk I'm seeing a future with so much potential in it. What a wonderful thing to see you moving into action!

- You are a leader really getting to know your own range—someone who's standing firm with your values and clear about your capabilities, someone whose actions are trustworthy by all who depend on you. It's wonderful to watch you.

- Some people develop one thing in coaching, some people develop a few things, and then there are those who unfold their full potential. What a pleasure to watch someone who is learning to unfold their full potential!

- Vision without action is merely a dream. Action without vision just passes the time. But some combine them. Watch out, now, because you're *really* getting started. Vision and action together can change the world!
- What a wonderful thing to realize that the past is behind you, and it's over. Yet who you are is the future you are living into. Your future belongs to you in every way. That's where you are truly developing your life. Relax and enjoy your dreams!
- Trust your vision thoroughly and completely. Enjoy your vision with real self-appreciation. Love your vision; it's your gift to the world!

Exercise: Cultivating a Range of Open-Ended Tones

In this exercise, you will practice using these open-ended coaching tones. Your task is to speak and practice like an actor thinking through an audition for an important part. You are opening up your range of expression and connection. Stand and speak to an important friend, someone who matters deeply to you. Imagine them in front of you. Read the practice lines again as if your well-being depends on it. Speak from the heart and get into the feeling tone of the message and its tonal quality. At first you might feel a little silly or artificial; however, you will find your authentic voice. The more you practice, the more you will be able to use your voice as an instrument to bring out the best in others.

First practice the three tones.

Notice how they are very different from each other.

Try sounding them out in a private coaching session with yourself. Then try the three positive tones with someone you care about.

- Speak clearly.

- Cultivate the ability to pace another person's volume, tone, tempo, and timbre. To do this, you must develop the ability to vary your voice, soft to loud, low to high.

- Cultivate emotional ranges in your voice: flat to passionate, questioning to declarative, high-pitched to deep.

If you are speaking in an environment with external noise, contrast your message with the noise by making it softer, slower, or deeper.

The Closed Tone: The Tone of the Warrior

Now that you have explored three expansive tones, we note one more. There is a fourth key tone, a closed tone that has a different function than the three open-ended tones. This fourth tone has the function of maintaining personal survival, against the odds. It is about taking action now. The inner voice is both determined and procedural. It requests that you take action to get through and survive.

The tone of the warrior tends to be pointed and direct. It may sometimes be sarcastic, and it may snarl at you. The message is either-or, the tone is flat.

The Assertion Function: The Tone of the Warrior

- Tactical, directive, focused, survival-oriented.

- Short, clear—giving instructions.

- Asserting necessity.

Examples

- Make it or break it.
- Sink or swim.
- No guts, no glory.
- No pain, no gain.
- Go big or go home.
- Put your money where your mouth is.
- Take no prisoners.
- Get it done or else.
- Winning isn't everything, it's the only thing.
- Failure is not an option.
- Get off the couch, and get your rear in gear.

As you can see, these are not gentle phrases. Most people use the tone of the warrior too often on themselves, day by day, and feel rather bruised. For most people, this internal dialogue may be peppered with inner conclusions. The warrior tone tends to be rather grim, tight, and serious. It instills the tension of no choice. The key is to learn how to shift gears and move from this tighter, tougher inner quality back to the other tones that allow people to relax and explore.

When is the warrior tone useful? We need this tone when the house is on fire or it's time to get into a hurricane shelter. We also may need it when it is time to step beyond an old, unnecessary habit.

This tone has value for survival actions, and it may also be useful when decisively deciding to do a difficult task that aligns with your highest vision. When the tone is used in this way, the warrior tone has the energy of a high five, where you passionately support a person to go further.

Here are some examples.

- You've set the actions. Time to put on your Nikes! Just do it!
- You're on track. Go for it!
- Okay, let's get it done!
- You're committed! Time to dive in!
- You go, girl!
- Time to step up and show yourself you can do it!
- Ready, set, go!

These statements are positive and supportive, yet it is important to recognize and understand when to use them appropriately. Most people respond best to warm tones of celebration and transformation. These tones allow people to relax and move to the next level.

Yet there are moments when the warrior tone can cut through an old trance. For this reason people may use the warrior tone to sound their inner fire alarm. The key is to know your clients well and do what works to champion them.

For yourself, it may be useful to remove the debilitating aspects of this tone from your own inner commentary and save it only for a few specific occasions where it is helpful—such as getting your tax forms ready when you are very tired or making a flight in time when you are running late, and so on.

What if it were possible, as a basic habit, to leave the unnecessary and tension-creating warrior voice on the beach of history and move into rich tonal openness of life? What if you could really experience and master the warm tones as part of who you are?

You can discover your voice as a vehicle for others' inner transformations. Move into the inner emotional territory celebrated by the tones of the wizard, the true friend, and the wise elder.

We summarize the tones briefly in Figure 5.1.

CHAPTER 5 *The Secret Tones of Transformation*

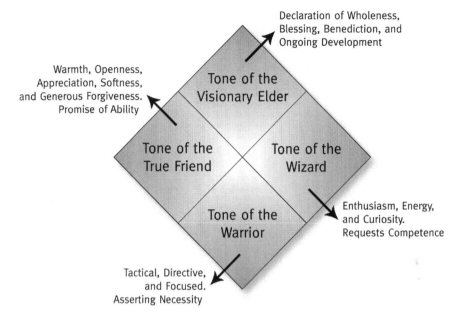

Figure 5.1: Four Creative Tones Functions.

The "I Love You" Exercise: Audio Practice

This is an exercise in noticing tonal qualities. The aim is to become aware of covert suggestions in daily life, such as those found in conversations, songs, written material, and advertising. This will help you become very clear and exact in your own tonal messages to your client.

This audio exercise is not a process, but simply an example of how using your voice changes the perception of your words.

- Compare the difference between the words "I love you!" when *shouted* and when *whispered*.

- Change the emphasis: **I** love you. I **love** you. I love **you**. Do you hear the difference?

- How about the pitch? Say "I love you!" in a *high, squeaky voice* and then *in a deep, low, voice*.

- Try the pacing: Say "I love you" very *fast* and then very *slow*.

- Now try the phrase in the tones of the wizard, the friend, the wise elder, and the warrior in the way you experienced using them in this chapter. Listen to the overtones and the inner messages. Now say it the way you want to, to someone you love.

As we become aware of the ways we can use our voices, our listening skills improve as well. As listening skills improve, we become stronger communicators. We have always found that the most beautiful communication takes place when we listen at a truly deep level that includes using our voice for more than just words.

Can you hear the thoughtfulness as you deliver these words?

Can you feel a sense of excitement now?

Can you feel it increasing as you read these words?

It's exciting to share these skills! As we become more sensitive to the communication that takes place beyond words, we are also more able to build rapport with matching voice tones and styles.

Practice the exercises in this chapter until you have a sense of control over your vocal tone and the moods and feelings you impart with your use of it.

Chapter 6

The Power of Framing and Committing

If you think you can, you can. If you think you can't, you're right.

—Mary Kay Ash

If you believe in something, no proof is necessary. If you don't, none is sufficient.

—Anonymous

The Story of Milton and the Calf

There was a large bull calf that had backed itself into a corner of the barn and refused to go outside with the rest of the herd. This was a healthy young animal, much stronger than the three boys attempting to pull it out by a rope around its neck. The boys pulled and pulled as hard as they could, but the calf pulled back harder, leaning back with its hooves fully set in the earthen floor. The standoff was totally balanced. Try as they might, the boys could not move the calf.

Milton, the oldest of the three boys, had an idea. While the other two pulled, he circled behind the barn, reached through a slot in the board wall, and pulled the calf by the tail further backward toward the back corner. Immediately the calf bolted in the other direction and ran out the door to freedom.

The calf's response was to oppose or move against any pull. Observing this and other habits with any person allows us to think about flexible ways to discuss, explore, interest, and motivate the person toward their own expressed wish for personal change.

CHAPTER 6 *The Power of Framing and Committing*

What Is a Frame? What Is Reframing?

"Powerful outcome creation" is a skill, and possessing and utilizing this skill is what distinguishes any consistently high performer from other performers. Framing is the skill of choosing how to look at a situation. You are then also creatively choosing the *meaning* of the situation. Your frame of reference or the meaning you choose, for a situation has a powerful effect on your later decisions and actions. A familiar example of framing is seeing the glass of water as half empty or half full.

You choose your frame. You determine if a situation is half empty or half full. If you choose the half empty frame of meaning, you look at what is missing and in turn attract more "half emptiness" into your life because of how you are focusing your mind. By choosing the half full frame of meaning and mind, you choose to look at what is working and what you have as a basis for moving forward and in turn attract more of what is working. Which would you like more of—fullness or emptiness?

We all know examples of people who are stuck in the half empty mentality.

- The woman in financial difficulty who chooses to focus on how hard it is to pay the bills instead of focusing on the vision she has for a prosperous life and what she might do to increase income.
- The child who wants the toy the other child has despite all the other toys he already has.
- The boss who is the constant critic, always complaining about what's wrong and never recognizing what's right.
- The man who chooses the victim stance, deciding that he has been wronged and focusing on how he has been held back.

Most individuals have been taught analysis thinking and problem solving, along with a focus on what is wrong or incorrect in a situation. Although problem analysis is deeply ingrained in our thinking, it is not the best approach to getting what we want. As long as we stay focused on the problem, *the problem itself* is the vision in our minds. The chronic thought of the problem produces bad feelings, and we end up attracting and creating more bad situations and bad feelings in our lives.

The quality of the questions you choose to ask a person, or yourself, are determined by your frame of reference. Within the half empty or half full frames are a number of inherent questions that lead your thoughts in a direction and these questions may or may not be serving you. You can choose to use questions that lead you to consider a frame that fills the glass, empties the glass, or even mixes the contents of the glass with something else in your desire. Exploring your desire is, in fact, another frame of the situation: "Do I want to have a glass that is empty, full, or mixed with something else?" These are all alternatives that lead our aim.

Often people do not stop to consciously consider the frame they are using in a situation. Their thoughts and feelings are on automatic and they believe that they have no control. What is the process by which the glass came to be half empty or half full in the first place? How did it become a habitual frame of reference?

We can really get turned around with questions such as "Who filled the glass? Who didn't fill the glass? What caused the glass to be there? Why did this happen?" These frames, though informative and interesting, can take you into a tailspin and are not at the heart of the coach approach to transformational communication because they do not directly focus on the solution. The heart of the coaching approach begins with a key question: "What are you truly aiming for? Why is it truly important to give this aim your energy?"

CHAPTER 6 *The Power of Framing and Committing*

Outcome Thinking

Developing an inspired vision of the future is the key to achieving what you want because you can only build what you can visualize. All things happen first in mind and then in reality. The skill of holding an outcome map in mind at all times leads the person toward their desired future. This is the primary step to start the magic of the coach approach.

To attain any goal or objective, no matter how big or small, the first thing you must do is identify specifically what you want. You must create a clear, inspiring, value-based vision of the desired outcome. This vision acts as a point of reference and provides the direction by which the transformational conversation will navigate.

If you are the coach, notice that all people want to be led by a future that inspires them, rather than being directed by a past that holds them back. For yourself, by drafting your unique dream you can move forward creatively. To start, you must get clear about four key aspects of the coaching approach.

- Where you are—your present state.
- Where you want to be—your desired state.
  (Focusing on this is the most important part.)
- The resources you need to move from one to the other.
- Your plan of action to narrow the gap between the present and the desired future.

With solution-focused coaching, outcome thinking of this nature is the basis of every conversation about direction and goal. With an outcome focus you support people (or yourself) to consciously fire up both the goal and the larger inspiring purpose beyond it. You help them get the big picture vision, the macro-vision, and then on to the micro-vision, moving through any important challenges. As described, setting the coaching focus is the first step. Together, you then contract to *do* what you say is important to do step by step.

Just like a good map naturally shows you the steps and checkpoints you will go through to reach a destination, the inspiring vision of your desired outcome is key to getting to where you want to go. Picturing the steps are important to achieving what you want. This naturally clarifies the process needed to arrive at the desired destination, while at the same time you remain open and resilient in handling the unexpected things that might come your way.

Transformational communicators use an outcome focus to support the person in evaluating if he or she is on track and taking action with the key steps. The person explores each step as needed to reach the goal. The coach encourages the client to build support structures, secondary routes, and contingency plans where required and have the unstoppable mindset that allows them to deal with anything that arises on the journey.

In other words, once the coaching conversation supports a person in getting clear about what he or she wants, it then supports the person in keeping that vision clearly in mind when determining and evaluating all the steps to reach it.

Find Elegant Solutions to Problems

Looking outside for fresh input is crucial. It sounds paradoxical, but we need to know what we don't know.

—John Kao

Imagine that you just received an unexpected complex problem and need to find a solution fast. You have never experienced this situation before. What is your approach? Most of us focus on the problem by asking questions such as: "Why do I have this problem? What shall I do to

CHAPTER 6 *The Power of Framing and Committing*

get rid of this problem? Are you sure this is my problem? Maybe it is someone else's."

Before you know it, the challenge becomes bigger by the minute. Your attention and effort are fully focused on overcoming the problem, and because whatever you put your attention on you get more of, you are attracting *more* of the problem. At the same time, you begin to feel less resourceful to find an acceptable (let alone elegant) solution.

When you focus on the problem instead of the desired outcome, you get stuck in the depths of the problem, as if you are in quicksand. Some people walk into the quicksand with lead boots on. One of the most powerful frames you can use to achieve results is to shift from a problem approach (I don't want X) to an outcome approach (What I want is Y). This immediately shifts your thinking and the way you feel.

This book shows you the skills involved with focusing on solutions and strengths at the very beginning of the conversation. You can master these skills by asking goal-focused questions that enable the ability to visualize. To this end, you can use the following solution-focused approach.

Shift your focus toward the positive. Examine your strengths, possible cooperation, and your resources.

Find openings toward solutions. Use scaling questions such as "What could move me one step forward—from a 3 to a 4 in terms of clarity?" Or, "Suppose I was beginning to experience the start of the solution, what would I be doing differently?"

Construct solutions. Use desired state questions such as *"What do I really want in this situation? What is my highest intention? What would be the very best result that I could achieve?"* What would need to be different for me to achieve this result? Spend time creating a vision of this outcome. See yourself already achieving this. As you visualize it, feel the feelings as if you had already achieved your aim.

Pretend to step into the future of having already achieved the outcome. As you feel the feelings of having achieved the goal, look back and see all the steps you took. Check the value. Here you are "future pacing" workability by checking the milestones that brought you to the best result.

Check how the solutions could work out. Use dissociated micro-visioning carefully. (You might try using a zoom lens to detail key steps, and if a step is not clear than go back to the vision and expect that the step will be revealed as you begin to take action. Be open to different paths.)

Ask if all elements have been studied to the point of taking effective action. You might scale up on a hypothetical effectiveness scale, weighing and checking the probable effectiveness of the key potential choices until the outcome is achieved.

Using the solution-focused approach, you will be surprised how competently you can tackle even the thorniest of problems and turn them into opportunities. To start with, choose a simple problem that you have been working on, one where you haven't yet found a solution. Follow the foregoing steps and discover how you find new solutions that can empower you.

Only when your frame of mind is changed to focusing on the desired result can you begin to move forward toward the desired outcome. People use this skill to float to fulfillment on wings of purpose.

An example of this is the high-performing salesperson who, when faced with difficult odds, decides to view the situation as an opportunity rather than an obstacle. Cheered by his outlook, he becomes a magnet to those around him who are inspired by his leadership. The result is a self-fulfilling prophecy. He outperforms against the odds with the support of those around him, cheering him on.

Solution-focused thinking habits magnetize our attention toward getting the desired outcome, and so the outcome is held in mind as the vision for the future. Others naturally tend to respond positively to our leadership because we hold the vision that serves everyone. Rather than dwelling on the difficulties or the setbacks, the idea of the solution becomes the royal road to results, and people feel cheered when they can see a strong pathway toward the solution and are inspired by the plan.

Imagine running a race where there are hurdles every 100 yards. With problem framing, you are focused on the hurdles, "Oh my, how high they are! How hard will I have to work to jump them?" Such a focus, with little or no attention on the finish line, will *not* make you a champion—guaranteed! The hurdles symbolically (and in reality) stand in your way. When you are focused on the hurdles, you cannot see past them to the finish line that is your true aim. The hurdles loom large in your mind, and the race seems difficult (if not impossible) to run.

The Key Skill that Makes the Difference in Transformational Communication

With a solution-focused approach, your mind is galvanized by your purpose and you are able to see past the hurdles before you. Your purpose always leads you to the finish line, and the hurdles become less important and less of an obstacle. In fact, they may seem so unimportant that they become nonexistent and are just part of the journey. They are still the same height. You'll still have to jump as high. Yet with the focus on the finish line, jumping the hurdles seems natural and easy. The end of the race is always drawing you onward. The race itself becomes a means to achieve the vision, and it's the vision—who you are becoming and who you are contributing to—that looms large in your mind. This difference in your focus is the power that leads you to success.

Notice how efficient this approach is. Solution-focused thinking is far more useful than problem-focused thinking, because the focus is on getting the desired outcome, rather than dwelling on the difficulties or setbacks. Constantly operating from a solution perspective is a noticeable characteristic of high achievers.

One of the main ways to producing solution-focused results that serve the world is to focus the mind and heart on who you are *becoming*—and not what you are *overcoming*. Allowing yourself to go into the lower energies of an overcoming focus puts you into a very challenging and unpleasant hurdle race. People can spend most of their lives running such a race.

As a transformational communicator using the coaching approach, once you are secure in this skill for yourself, you will quickly discover the value of using it consistently in coaching conversations with others. This simple and subtle skill of flipping a problem or conflict into a solution-focused orientation may be the single most powerful characteristic of transformational coaches who support integral change.

When outcomes are declared and visualized carefully, people move toward them naturally, almost effortlessly. What was once considered a problem is now little more than a pebble on the road! Having a strong, inspiring, value-based vision for the future cuts all other concerns down to size.

Once you, the transformational communicator, know how to consciously assist people to orient toward their larger purpose and goals, your clients will move consistently and more easily toward their desired outcomes. They will achieve their outcomes by *choice,* not by *chance*.

Developing, holding, and feeling a vision of a compelling future is the single most important task for a person, in order to achieve their goals and dreams.

Without this vision and consistently visualizing it, people move in a random, scattered fashion. They are likely to struggle and get frustrated and stuck.

Chapter 6 The Power of Framing and Committing

When people make the choice to hold a specific outcome securely on the movie screen of their minds, they naturally begin to move toward making their vision a reality—no matter how large or small it is. Their chosen outcome becomes their future.

Who you are is the future you are moving into. What is in your mind becomes your reality. You have two choices. You can visualize how your problems continue, which will move you towards having even more problems. Or, you can visualize your outcome becoming real and move toward having it. Which do you prefer?

The Outcome Exercise

Try this exercise for a personal understanding of what it means to hold an outcome focus.

On a piece of paper, list five to ten difficult situations you have handled successfully.

Then, on another piece of paper, list five to ten difficult situations that you didn't handle so well.

Go down each list and after each situation note whether you were more focused on the problem or on the outcome. Ask yourself: "Did I know what I wanted? How clear was my intended outcome? Was I really stating it as a positive result, something in my control?"

Although there are often other variables that affect your results, you will probably find that the successful situations were ones in which you used an outcome focus and you had a clear, specific goal in mind. Notice and clarify to what extent your success is related to you having a clear vision, an effective outcome frame. Do you usually think about getting results this way?

Review the unsuccessful list. Did the less effective result happen when the aim(s) were less clear to you or seemed in some ways out of your control?

How can you use this personal inventory to assist you with some present goals?

Chapter 7

Contracting: Setting the Focus of the Conversation

Imagination is everything. It is the preview of life's coming attractions.

—Albert Einstein

The great thing in this world is not so much where we stand, as in what direction we are moving.

—Oliver Wendell Holmes Sr.

Engagement and Power in Superstition Mountains

I have never really been afraid of starting out on an exploratory venture in the wild country. When I was eight years old, I loved to walk out and visit the shepherds and their flocks miles into the hills near the California town where my family briefly lived. Since childhood I have found the chance to wander off into the hills to be a sweet freedom.

I took the opportunity several times when I lived in Arizona. Close to my home lay the huge wilderness of the Superstition Mountains in the Nevada highlands, an area with multiple mountain ranges, amazing rock formations, strange cacti and plants, hundreds of trails, hidden springs, and rich wildlife.

Starting out on a five-day hike one early spring day, I revisited beautiful areas I had seen before and continued into new territory. One day later I was in an area that seemed wild and desolate. After crossing a rocky highland I entered a large valley with some grass and trees. I noticed that there were many animal prints in the dried soil. While walking down the trail I saw more and more prints, all seeming to be from different types and sizes of animals. I carried neither tent, weapon, nor matches, so I sat down to drink some juice and consider the situation. The sun began to set.

The beautiful valley was very quiet, and I considered my options. It had been a long day, and it seemed so easy to pull out my sleeping bag and lie down in the valley of the footprints and get a good night's sleep, feeling safe and secure. However, this place had a distinctly strange feel to it, and I felt troubled and uncertain.

Turning back was very risky at this time of the evening. To reach this place I had spent an hour on the trail crossing a very rocky, windy

CHAPTER 7 Contracting: Setting the Focus of the Conversation

highland. To go back now as darkness descended seemed foolhardy. It was a long way to climb to leave this valley.

I vividly remember that moment, asking myself to focus on alternatives carefully while pondering my choices. The best spot to stay in the valley didn't seem clear . . . there were dried footprints everywhere in puzzling array. What animals? What to do?

Suddenly I saw him. He looked like a small dog watching me from the side of a nearby hill. I realized it was a coyote. He was sitting quietly, very relaxed on his haunches, observing me with interest. Then, without looking back, he trotted over the hill and out of sight.

No problem, I thought, it's just one small coyote. But the vast array of footprints held my gaze. Many and different animals had been here. What to do?

The idea came like a flash. As a girl I had read about the territorial practices of wolves in Never Cry Wolf by Farley Mowatt. He described how the wolves in the northern Canada always respected the boundaries of his camp if he "peed the borders" of his territory. Focus turned into intention and I thought to myself, "What a good idea! Let's test it." I spent at least an hour consuming enough liquid to do the job and sorting out my boundaries. I made them rather close, given the required amount of fluid. I then laid down to sleep.

I would love to tell you that I had a quiet night. Not on your life!

I woke up to see a vast array of stars in the darkness and to hear the bush crashing with moving animals and an orchestra of sounds—barks, yelps, and rustles everywhere. It was surely the national convention of the coyotes in my small valley, and I was certainly a prize exhibit. One group howled from one side of the valley, and the howls were picked up with barks all round. Again and again I heard animals come and stir around my camp, though clearly none

107

came passed my carefully marked borders. I lay there rather stiffly, with only my nose poking from the bag.

Finally the noise stopped and the dawn arrived. It was not my best night of sleep, but I arose thankful and alert that my inner questioning had brought me to safety and I could now dust myself off and greet the day.

I was a city slicker in the wilderness, yet the power of focused attention had allowed me to communicate to the pack and be respected. The story sometimes seems like a joke, but I remind myself that the capacity to find good ideas when you need them is far from a laughing matter. I had asked myself: "What do I want to achieve, and how might I achieve that?" My inner response, from the depth of my being, rewarded me with an empowered plan.

Our creative capacity to solve problems in surprising ways is what most defines us as humans. My solution was just a small amusing idea from a book read twenty years earlier, but it was exactly what was needed for the moment. I find it amazing that clear ideas landed between my ears when I focused and inwardly asked for help. Since then, this tale has reminded me that all of us can find the exact answers we need.

This capacity informs my faith in humanity. Each of us are capable of focus and action and can find the solutions that are able to bring our species through the dark times and into the fullness of our human powers.

CHAPTER 7 *Contracting: Setting the Focus of the Conversation*

The Power of Contracts

The foundation of a transformational conversation is built when we are fully present with a person, establishing rapport and operating in clear focus with the person's model of the world. When this foundation is present, the next step is to set the focus and outcome for the conversation. We call this process *contracting*. This is a verbal contract, set in the moment between client and coach at the beginning of the conversation. Note that this is very different than the written business contract outlined at the start of the business arrangement between coach and client. Verbal contracting at the start of a coaching conversation is an essential element of solution-focused coaching because it gives form to the coaching journey so the coach and client know if they are on track.

Contracting Sets the Intention and Attention of Powerful Coaching

The coaching partnership or transformational conversation needs to start strong. A verbal contract is a powerful beginning, like an archer pulling back the bow of attention with a strong arm. The aim of our intention sets the focus, and the contract is the mental picture of where that arrow will go. An effective contract is the arm of intention. Through the conversation, this arm sends the arrow forth and the deeper-knowing mind responds by opening up the creativity bank with a flow of ideas. We declare our intention for the conversation, and set the contract. Like the archer, we shoot the arrow with focused questions.

This often surprises people, because they don't know their own power until the intention is fully set. Once the coaching focus or contract is set, a strong transformational communicator will enter coach position and stay there for the duration of the conversation.

For an archer with a bow, all his power and focus must come together as he evaluates the full distance of his first moment's aim. Only then can he start getting clear on the lay of the land—in other words, the steps required to determine where the arrow will hit. You cannot have a transformational conversation where there is integral change without such a clear focus for the conversation.

Using the Contracting Question to Set the Focus

The "agreement to accomplish XYZ," the basic contracting question, is best established in the first moments of every coaching conversation. When you use a contracting question to set the focus of a conversation, the client can continuously check the value of the conversation to see if he or she is on track. If you are using these skills as a coach, as a manager (one on one, or in a group setting such as a team meeting) or in an intimate relationship, you can set the process with a contract question that will move you toward deep rapport and flow.

The contracting question sets the focus for the conversation and moves you toward rapport and flow.

For those applying these skills as a professional coach, you should understand that establishing the focus for the conversation marks the formal beginning of the coaching session. In both cases, the specific contracting question you use is very important because it sets the agenda for the conversation.

To establish a contract well, we need to contract both for the focused energy and the focused time frame of our client. To set a strong contract, you might say something like the following.

Chapter 7 Contracting: Setting the Focus of the Conversation

"What would be the best possible result you would get from our forty-five minutes together?"

"We have twenty-five minutes together today. What do you believe would be the most important thing to achieve today?"

"What do you believe is the best use of our conversation this morning? We have thirty minutes. What would you like to accomplish?"

We have twenty minutes together. What is the best outcome you are looking for that is within your control to achieve?"

Notice that each contract specifies the time range and requests the goal range by asking for the *best possible result.* Each example focuses the conversation by maintaining total responsibility for the results produced in the allocated time. The clients hold the frame for what they produce, and they know the name of the game. *They* are responsible to step up and create a result within their control, while you, the coach, hold the space for them. (Remember, your role is not to produce the result for them. Your job is to awaken the genius within them that already has the resources to be a success.)

The power of the primary coaching contract affects the quality of a coaching session very deeply. If a coach obtains an agreement from the client to achieve a result in forty-five minutes, the client will often have great insights in the last fifteen minutes of the session. If the contract agreement is for thirty minutes, the client will often make discoveries that are timed perfectly. The same is true for the brief sessions of a strong "walkabout" managerial coach dropping by to talk with various members of his staff, usually for less than ten minutes, as he asks them, "How's it going?" I compare a person's great questions to the function of an excellent electrician, connecting everyone into flow states that get them reinspired.

The trust of the client is deepened when contracts are regularly and dependably set at the beginning of a conversation, once the rapport is in place. The client quickly learns to trust that how he or she wants to spend the time is considered the most important focus of the conversation. This certainty of support allows people to appreciate the coaching process so that they focus on their deepest level of participation in each conversation.

Throughout the conversation, a contract question gives your clients the certainty that you are on track as a conversational partner and that you are deeply interested in what is important to them. Then they can relax and proceed in the conversation with confidence in your presence.

From Abstract to Specific: 50,000-Feet Contracts to 50-Feet Contracts

An important quality of a coaching conversation could be compared to altitude. The metaphor of altitude is useful because it very much determines how we support the client and how we track relevance. We get results, as directed by the client, at the detail level that is needed for the specific goal. Clients know the level of specificity they need, so ask them and measure the clarity of the actions agreed on according to the level of specificity really needed.

As you get better at assisting people in selecting clear, actionable goals you may notice that all goals tend to be organized around one of at least three different levels of specificity.

- Some goals, such as clarifying a mission or exploring potential long-term plans, are 50,000-feet goals. The action result remains very high even though the person may organize the steps. These 50,000-feet goals may also be "being" goals that focus on developing qualities or inner states that translate to all areas of life.

- Some goals, such as organizing the completion of a project over several months, might be considered as operating at the

5,000-feet level. We can see their outlines clearly and specify areas of detailing and organizing.

- Other goals, such as designing and organizing the action items needed for a specific meeting, are 50-feet level goals. These are very detailed and specific.

The key element in effective coaching is that clients *do* take action so they manifest exactly what they want. A good coach supports the alignment of thoughts, feeling, and *actions*.

It is very important to make sure your client's outcome for the session is specific enough to produce the result he or she wants. Many beginner coaches get caught working with a contract that may seem much too large to organize into relevant action areas, and that match the scope of the session arranged.

For example, if the person wants to pick a topic for their doctoral degree and then plan all the chapters in one coaching conversation or session, the coach needs to be willing to vigorously challenge the request. One might ask questions like the following.

- What then would be the most valuable *beginning step or steps* that you would like to accomplish in *this* session?

- "To write the doctoral dissertation just the way you want, what would be the very best result from today's thirty minutes to *start* this process?

Effective Contracting Considerations

There are several considerations to keep in mind when setting a contract at the beginning of a coaching session.

1 The client may need time to clarify the most important and most relevant thing to work on in the ses-

sion. In some situations the client may spend a whole session getting the contract specific enough to coach around. Of course you are encouraged to aim to get the contract as soon as possible, and supporting the client's process is very important.

2   Notice the current level of the contract. Then ask yourself, "According to *this* level, do we have an actionable contract?" Some contracts are naturally overview contracts at the 50,000-feet level (for example, creating a great mission or overviewing a long-range plan). Some contracts are naturally 5,000-feet contracts (designing capabilities and actions for the next project, for example). Some are 50-feet contracts. "I would like to write a list of action steps and priorities for this week."

3   Be certain to work with the client to clarify the level of specificity he or she desires as an outcome before moving into the coaching session. Never assume what the client wants. *Ask!* It is very valuable to get clear on what the client will see, hear, and feel at the end of the coaching session that proves it was the best use of his or her time.

Listening for a Creator, Reactor, or Visitor

Focus on where you want to go, not on what you fear.

—Anthony Robbins

In a transformational conversation, you create a relationship with the client that requires both of you to be fully present. All communication is a dance of exploration, so a true transformational conversation is an exploration by two people together. This means it requires a person as a client that is clear on what she wants and is willing to do the work to get it; willing to look at herself, her goals, her deeper meaning, and her rela-

CHAPTER 7 Contracting: Setting the Focus of the Conversation

tionships in a new way. Without the desire to genuinely make progress, a person will not take action.

We have mentioned the emotional brain (see volume 1) and difficulties people may have with already developed emotional conclusions and habits. Sometimes a negative frame of mind or limiting conclusions will arrive as soon as a person begins to speak. Even as she begins to imagine a powerful intention for the conversation the gremlins fly in to roost: "I can't . . . I don't like . . . I don't want . . . I'm not capable . . . He's so . . . "

The person, in the moment, is caught by negative framing and inner conclusions and registering these feelings in his or her body. When clients start to speak about what isn't working, what won't work, or what they don't want, they paint themselves into a corner with complaints and negative beliefs. This must be dealt with before a coaching conversation can really happen because energy flows to where a person's attention goes. People become and manifest what they think and feel about. Negative imaging and bad feelings require immediate notice because these conclusions will cork the bottle of possibility. A transformational communicator quickly develops skills in interrupting this process and supports the client to reframe his or her thinking.

If a negatively framed response or complaint comes forth, notice from coach position what stops the client from being able to set his or her intention *this* moment. As a coach who will work with many different people, you will notice a range of intentional muscles from very limp to strong. Some people have temporary stops on the path. Others claim to have no intentional path at all.

At the outset of the conversation, you might notice three types of responses given by people who enter a conversation with you. The response the person gives has him or her enter a temporary category. We call them visitors, reactors (complainers), and creators. These categories are cartoony. The distinctions are only shared to allow us to develop appropriate strategies for the type of responses and the conversational approaches that might be required to best support the person on any particular day.

Let us backtrack and summarize our process to this stage. After you have built rapport and the person has agreed to the coaching conversation, you ask a contracting question: "We have about thirty minutes together. If this was the best use of your time and you had the best possible result from our conversation, what would that be?" After this question, you enter coach position and listen structurally to what the person has to say. You listen for his or her response and notice the type of focus and aim that the person takes.

Visitors

A client may have been *told* or otherwise directed to have a conversation with you. (For instance, an employee sent by a manager or a teenager sent by a parent). Perhaps an advisor, friend, or supervisor has suggested they talk with you. Without buy-in from the client to have the transformational conversation that allows for a desired change, the person may be only a *visitor*.

Visitors do not have a desire to change things. A visitor may not recognize a need for change because they do not have a goal to achieve or a challenge to solve. The person may be locked in a struggle for control of results with the person who sent them to the session. The person may also have a belief or expectation that change is not possible. People with deeply private concerns or hidden addictions can also be found in this category.

If you have a conversation with a visitor, look for and compliment their strengths and positive points. Be warm and genuinely interested in their model of the world. Occasionally they will decide to engage in a truly authentic conversation and begin to speak with you in a heartfelt way. Through the power of your warm questions, you can find what is most important to them. They might discover the personal value that would inspire them and move them toward the change they want. Notice that if they walk away, they were never a client. We simply say hello, engage in a few shared moments, congratulate them for honoring whoever sent them, and say good-bye.

Reactors

Reactors have a complaint and a desire to achieve a goal by altering things, yet because they focus on what they do not want, they are not ready to take the necessary action to get the result. They may be creating negative movies in their mind. They may believe what they want is too difficult or impossible to achieve. These people can easily fill your time with complaining because they do not believe it is possible to create the integral change that they wish.

Notice that they want results but don't know how to get them. They have forgotten their true focus and have listened to their inner fears or doubts or other emotional conclusions about themselves or others. Before this person can begin a true coaching conversation, he or she needs to take aim again.

There are often several layers of doubts: "Maybe I can't, maybe he won't let me, or maybe it's too much work." Even beyond that: "What if I begin and then fail?" The transformational conversation is what moves people through these layers and back to the power of their original intention. Your questions can gently take the person back to his or her original intent.

This is often an intense and powerful conversation with a person who is deciding again on the value of his or her aim and purpose. Your questions and support help the person get back into the transformational flow of his or her own original aim. This conversation offers emotional release. If people regain their aims, they will emerge into the inner sunlight and positive emotions of their own hearts' desires.

If you have a reactor or complainer in a conversation, ask the person to think of something they want to have happen. For example, you might say, "If you don't want *XYZ*, what *do* you want instead?" Another good question might be, "What do you want from this situation that is within your control to do something about?"

Creators

When a person is truly ready and willing to do something about a desired aim they are a *creator*. In fact, to truly complete the conversation, you need a creator. Otherwise we work with only beginning explorations.

You will find that creators are inspired and motivated by what they want and just need to figure out how to make it happen. You must have a creator—someone who knows what they want and is willing to do what it takes to get it—to have a transformational conversation. The person with whom you are connecting must state what they want in the positive, it must be within their control to do something about, and they must know how they will know if they have achieved it.

Creators state what they want in the positive, it is within their control to do something about, and they know how they will know if they have achieved it.

The Five Criteria of a Good Contract

When the client answers your contracting question and states what he or she wants from the coaching session, you want to listen for the response sounding something like the following:

- Stated in the positive: "I want . . ."
- Within the person's control to do something about.
- Truly meaningful and important to the person.
- Specific, measurable, achievable, realistic/relevant, and timed for completion (SMART goals).
- Clear how the coach and client will know when the outcome is achieved. This means the coach and client are clear on the evidence procedure (i.e., understand what the client will see, hear, and feel at the end of the coaching session that demonstrates the outcome was achieved).

SMART Goals are

- **S**pecific
- **M**easurable
- **A**chievable
- **R**ealistic and relevant
- **T**imed for completion

If you notice that a contract is missing a few of these elements, ask powerful questions that support revealing these items.

Here are some sample questions that can achieve this.

- So you don't want to fight with your husband. What *do* you want?
- What do you want in your relationship with your husband that is within your control?
- On a scale of 1 to 10, how important is improving your relationship with your husband right now? What value will this offer your life? Why is it so important?
- What specifically do you want to achieve in this area in the next thirty minutes?
- What would you walk away with today that proved you had made an inner shift to approach your marriage in a new way?

Complaining Pattern Awareness

Humans can slip into the lower energies and shame, blame, and complain about ourselves or others from time to time. It is an interesting thing to explore our complaint habits. Where do you tend to complain in your life? Do you ever complain about yourself? Or do you mostly complain about others? Do you grumble privately to yourself? Or do you speak out to others?

Everyone has their favorite topics for complaining! Bad drivers, bad weather, bad friends, bad habits, bad jobs, bad bosses, bad roads, bad food, bad computer programs, bad traffic jams, lack of time, lack of money, lack of support, lack of focus, lack of energy, lack of effective training, lack of abilities, lack of results, lack of completion . . .

What fires up the complaint tone for you?

How do you speak your complaints?

Do you speak cause/effects? (This causes this!)

Do you use universals? (This always happens! This never happens!)

Do you speak expectations? (This kind of person or situation can usually be expected to produce these bad results in this particular way.)

Do you use a tone of resignation, anger, indignation, frustration, sadness, or cynicism?

Do you complain by labeling? Someone or something is too sloppy, too neat, too expensive, too poor, too tall, too short, too fat, too thin, too rich, too smart, too stupid, and so on.

Labeling is interesting. We divide the world into people or situations that are either in the category or outside of it. For example, if you complain and say that someone is very unprofessional, you divide all human beings into two camps: those who are professionals and those who are not professionals. These are labels. A great divide is created if a label says a person is a certain quality. An "is" quality is at the level of identity; an "is" quality never changes, by definition.

This also means that the unconscious mind, which naturally expresses the team quality of the emotional brain, treats all people as one and the same. This means that we need to pay close attention to our messages because our unconscious minds treat all messages, both positive and negative, as only about the self. Whatever labels we apply to others are like mirrors: They are actually about ourselves.

I invite you to ponder this question: How might you hear the tone of your complaint in a creative way, so you do not get pulled into the inner tone of the complaint, the mode of the complaint, and the posture of the complainer? How might you live your life as a magnificent creator instead?

CHAPTER 8

The Four Essential Questions in Coaching

Our personal power is found in the force of our thoughts—it is our real freedom!

—Anonymous

Learning How to Walk

Milton Erickson used to tell a powerful story about his first days after getting ill with polio as a boy. He discusses the inspiring idea he got that changed his life in a very positive way. Being sick became a springboard to some of his greatest questions and lessons.

Imagine being a fifteen-year-old boy who went to bed one evening with a sore throat and woke up three days later after nearly dying from polio. What would it be like for you if you discovered you could only move your eyes—that you were, in fact, paralyzed? That is a situation that Milton experienced and lived through as a young man.

In the 1930s, medical authorities in rural areas of the United States didn't know what to do with a very ill young boy like Milton. They simply helped his mother make a bed in the kitchen so he could be near her as she worked. There he lay, day after day, watching his mother at her daily tasks, busy with a newborn baby and a toddler.

Milton wished desperately to be able to move, and longingly watched and observed his newborn sister raising her head and lowering it. Because of his deep desire to regain his own mobility, he began to imagine himself being able to do that simple move, and, surprisingly, after a few visualizations, he experienced some faint movement in his neck muscles. With glee, he visualized again and again and got more movement. He realized he was on to something: He began a daily routine, hour after hour, observing his sister becoming familiar with her movements, and doing exactly what he saw her do in his mind's eye.

Month after month he continued with this daily visualization. As the baby learned to raise her hands, kick her legs, and so on, he practiced her techniques mentally. Then, as the skills started to come back faintly, he practiced physically.

Two years later, after rigorous visualization and practice, Milton was able to walk using two canes. The doctors considered it a miracle; he considered it hard work.

According to current authorities, Milton had rebuilt his damaged nerve pathways by using new brain territory. Some equated his new abilities to what babies are able to do if they have experienced brain damage before the age of six months. Milton noticed that the process required was asking himself key questions while he visualized again and again.

The result for Milton was twofold. He not only regained a large degree of his lost capability but created the opportunity to deeply understand the power of awareness, observation, question asking, purpose exploration, visualization, and rapport. These well-practiced understandings gradually allowed him first to walk, then to finish high school, and later to begin a highly successful and creative medical career. He had acquired robust capacities to observe, question, and follow inner cues—capacities that most people never develop over a lifetime.

The Power of Full Intention to Bring Us to Full Value

Consider the possibility that ideas that occur to us have a process life of their own. When we enter a transformational conversation, it is as though we are putting on the skis of a good idea to swiftly move around the slopes of the mind. Milton's experience shows how powerfully modeling and simple visualization can create holographic imprints and process understandings in the body-mind.

Such an imprint is a strong model of visual, tonal, and other simple habit linkage. An example might be the habit of automatically moving your foot to the brake when the tail lights from a car in front of you flash red.

Milton's story demonstrates how deeply our thoughts and our physical experience are connected. It is a wonderful discovery that he could observe his baby sister and, by visualizing the successful implementation of the skills she was mastering, could transform his own abilities. Clearly, through visualization and focus you, too, can realize your authentic capabilities and begin to trust them in ways that will change your life.

The Personal Reach Exercise

Let's try a little exercise together to demonstrate the powerful visualizing capacities of the cerebral cortex.

Stand up and face forward. Reach your right arm out to the side, parallel with the ground. Point your finger. Keeping your hips facing forward, turn from the waist and bring your left arm and head around to the right toward the extended arm as far as you can comfortably turn. Make note of how far you have turned by noticing where your finger is pointing. Repeat three times (switching right to left), to establish just how far you can comfortably turn.

Close your eyes and imagine yourself turning without actually moving. See yourself turning farther than you did before. Repeat three times visually in your mind's eye.

With your eyes closed, turn as far as you comfortably can. Holding the position, open your eyes and note how much farther you have turned, just by visualizing it!

Inspiring ideas linked to effective visualization and transformational conversation can truly provide magical, integral development. By visualizing you become able to create wonderful flow states of choice as well as changes that catalyze your ideas and experiences and create real-world results.

"Flow" Conversations: A Fluid Model

The flow of ideas can become even more alive in a transformational conversation. The powerful open-ended questions of a coach can continue to develop more ideas successfully and reorganize the closet of your mind. Observing four aspects of any goal encourages the flow of our ideas and keeps effective ideas emerging out of the closet and into the open air. We can then observe the content, structure, process, and the long-range form of these developing ideas. (More will be shared on this topic in Book Three of this series: *Process and Flow*.)

How do you amplify the value of your own good ideas? Occasionally, as in the story of Milton's inspiration with his baby sister, our best ideas come in a moment of awakened awareness, like an inspiration or like a gift. When we use them and test them, we learn their value experientially and they become part of us. More frequently, they emerge by asking purposeful outcome or goal-directed questions, which we need to persist in pursuing. We need to explore through time if we are to find the value.

Questions Are the Answer

Focusing on outcomes allows you to have a visceral conversation with your own life and get in touch with your strongest purposes and goals. Suppose you could have such a dialogue with life: What does *life* want from you?

When coaches step back, relax, and wonder about the really important questions for our clients, magic starts to occur. People often begin to deeply ponder their core value questions. This basic theme comes up so often in coaching conversations that it seems as if life wants us to ponder our fundamental aims, find our deepest questions, really *ask* them purposefully, and know that the answers are within!

It seems as if people need to call forth their core questions, the biggest questions that they have. People seem to know innately that the quality of the questions they ask inwardly determines the quality of their lives. Some people climb mountains and ask the wind. Some people sit in a cave and ask the darkness or the spark of light. Some people sing their questions, others dance them. How do you contact your really important questions? How do the answers tend to be revealed to you?

In this chapter we encourage you to move yourself curiously into the exploration of your own real purpose and use these key ideas to start a conversation. We invite you to use the coaching processes to explore your own heart. Notice as a self-coach that it's *only* when you ask your own important questions inwardly and with real focus that your inner life can rise up and speak to you.

Four Engaging Questions That Support the Unfolding of Any Project

Think back to your experience with the personal reach exercise. Your goal reach is like your physical reach: It can be stretched. It connects strongly to the size of your inspiration, how important you make the goal, and your willingness to persist and keep discovering ways to get there.

You may want to visualize a baseball diamond with the batter coming in for a home run. We will explore four basic engaging and planning questions that support the batter moving around the diamond. The diamond can represent the four key stages in any plan and its fulfillment. These are the stages of first, inspiration; second, implementation; third, commitment; and finally, completion and satisfaction (see Figure 8.1).

CHAPTER 8 *The Four Essential Questions in Coaching*

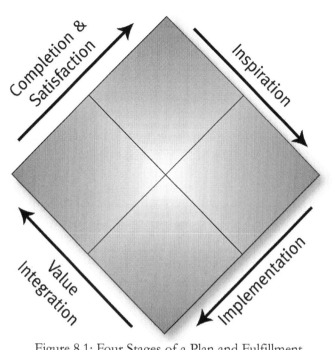

Figure 8.1: Four Stages of a Plan and Fulfillment.

Four engaging questions connect with these stages. They help a person build a vision around these stages of achievement. These planning questions focus or frame the conversation toward the person's desired results at each stage. By starting with a version of these four directional questions, all the criteria of a well-specified outcome gradually becomes part of the discussion and begins to be organized.

The four questions, which may be verbalized in different ways, can be used as an interlinked group, each one assisting with the next. Together, these questions can lead you and the people you coach to an inspired vision of the future. These directional questions are the foundation of solution-focused coaching and therefore the basis of transformational conversations. Let us look at them closely.

Question 1: What Do You Want?

We start with creating clarity around where the person is and exactly what the person really wants. This exploration starts the coaching conversation. When you are clear on what you want, you are inspired to achieve and have motivation to work. You can work through the secondary questions that arise whenever you have a goal to work toward. A clear and compelling vision of the desired outcome motivates, stimulates, and excites people. This provides the energy and impetus to take action. This is necessarily the beginning point in any transformational conversation.

WHAT DO YOU WANT? Variations

- What are you aiming for here?
- What do you wish to achieve?
- What are you going for now?
- What is your main goal for this conversation?
- What results do you want to get today?
- What is your intentional outcome for the next thirty minutes?
- What are you called or guided to step up to today?
- What would you absolutely love to accomplish?

Every version of this question, "What do you want?," tends to encompass some additional questions to support the clarity and inspiration that can make the vision a reality. Also implied in the question "What do you want?" is the *why*, or value, behind the outcome. You want a specified outcome because it has *value* to you. You are naturally exploring what the achievement is a means toward? What might be the goal behind the goal? What is your highest intention? An effective coach will hold this key frame with careful attention to all aspects of each aim the client presents.

The deeper value behind a goal and the feelings linked to it is what the person really wants to achieve, and this also requires focus. The goal itself is a means of reaching that deeper value. By understanding the person's need to live the deeper value, the goal becomes even more meaningful for them. Just as a rosebud unfolds as it opens to its full beauty, showing more layers of petals until the final glory is revealed, so do each person's goals have deeper layers of meaning and achievement.

As you listen to another person discuss what he or she wants, encourage an outcome statement that is worded in the positive and in the client's control. Imagine a checklist in your mind. What does the person want on the deepest level that is within her control?

This question also encourages the visualization of the ultimate outcome. The key is to hold this image in your awareness and repeatedly visualize your desires and goals as already being fulfilled. Feel the feelings you would feel if you had already manifested your desire. The intensity of the feeling is what supports you magnetizing what you want.

Question 2: How Might You Get It?

As the person holds the clear vision, the next question for beginning a plan of action is one that asks *how* he or she will successfully achieve the goal. This typically involves subgoals or mini-goals that build into the desired outcome step by step. The careful consideration of a plan of action in bite-size pieces makes all the difference because reviewing the details makes the vision appear more achievable.

In addition, seeing each small step adds more elements to the detail of what the person truly wants, deepening the person's involvement in his or her vision and the wonderful journey toward it. As you move forward with these engaging questions, the discussion stimulates the person's motivation to successfully complete what they are starting.

HOW MIGHT YOU GET IT? Variations

- How will this be achieved?

- How can this happen?

- What might be the master plan to achieve this?

- What are some of the best ways you can get this to unfold most effectively?

- What are the steps that will get you from where you are to where you want to go?

- How might you begin to make this happen?

Encompassed in these questions are the questions of *who* the person will have to *be* or *become* to achieve their goal. What will the person need to *do* to reach this outcome? What capabilities and skills need to be developed? What *resources* will the person want to find? *How* can these resources be turned into achievement of the goal?

This question also encourages the visualization of timelines and steps. What is the first step the person must take to achieve the desired outcome? What is the second step? What is the third? Each step should lead cumulatively to the achievement of the desired outcome.

The acronym of **SMART** goals can be a great help here. Remember from Chapter 7 that **SMART** means **s**pecific, **m**easurable, **a**chievable, **r**ealistic/relevant, and **t**imed for completion. As you design coaching questions, run this acronym through your attention and mentally check all components. This awareness develops your coaching effectiveness.

Often at this stage, we move to question 4 because it helps us clarify and develop micro-vision more clearly toward a specified, measurable, knowable result.

Question 3: How Might You Deepen Your Commitment?

This third question area encompasses many questions. It is about taking the plan further and making it more meaningful. This always calls for pondering and deep consideration. How deep is your commitment to your dream? How might you take your plan further? How might you strengthen or expand your commitment? How might you truly make this happen? How might you really be certain to move forward? How might you make the journey more meaningful for yourself and others?

Other questions that might be important to consider are: "What will allow your plan to naturally and easily unfold? How might you accomplish these action steps more effectively and efficiently? How would you overcome an obstacle that could come your way? What obstacles might show up, and how can you solve them in advance?"

> ***HOW MIGHT YOU DEEPEN YOUR COMMITMENT?* Variations**
>
> - What is important to learn on this journey?
> - How might you move even further?
> - What are you deeper performance goals with this achievement?
> - What will unfold for you out of getting these results?
> - How can you make the journey more meaningful for yourself and others?
> - Can you see higher level results from committing to this? What might they be?

By making longer range plans, you consider the possibility that your first plan might not work and prepare for this eventuality. Making long-range plans confirms your commitment to see the desired outcome through, even if circumstances appear to conspire against you. This cycles you back to question 2, and you might ask, "What other ways might I get what I want?"

Visualizing how the goal might lead to higher level results also sets the stage for effective consideration of the best plans to accomplish the outcome. Should circumstances change, the person is prepared with multiple options to move forward and remain true to the original value-based vision that inspired them in the first place. There are many roads that lead to a chosen destination; we must notice our journey carefully. Detours, then, are only that—detours. A recognized commitment keeps us from veering off course.

Achieving the destination is still possible despite roadblocks in certain areas. By considering questions such as, "How might I overcome any roadblock someone else presents?" and "How might I move past any roadblock I create for myself? What is my contingency plan?," the person develops a personal map of alternative routes.

The map of alternate routes becomes especially useful when the wider ecology is considered. This person learns to examine all the consequences of reaching the outcome successfully, as well as the consequences of the chosen action plans. He or she learns to consider the wider consequences? How will this affect other areas of his or her life? Is there anything that he or she will have to give up or change to achieve this outcome? Does *not* having this outcome benefit him or her? How will he or she deal with that benefit when observing that the outcome is actually achieved? They also need to consider who else is affected and how they will feel as they move their goal toward completion.

We are looking at subtle questions here that may or may not seem to be in the person's control. The ways people tend to be stopped often have to do with relationship issues of some sort. Think about specific situations for yourself: For you to achieve your desire, you may have to give up old beliefs, and hence your relationship with yourself may change. You also may have to change how you relate to others to truly achieve your outcomes.

Each person is different and needs a customized approach. Vision and first steps go hand and hand. We don't need to see all the bends in the road. We just need to see that our road is real, available, and can be effectively tracked. *Then* begin!

This means that on a basic, core level you realize that you *will* do it. You just need to know that you *are* going to get there. This is the power of holding a vision of your final destination and expecting that you will be guided to find the way with your inner GPS. Hold the vision and feel the feelings of having already achieved it, and you will be surprised and dazzled by what shows up in your life.

The I.A.M. Formula
Intention + Attention = Masterful Manifestation

Let's break this down. *Intention* is something you decisively decide on for your future. Your intention is what you choose to create for yourself and others. It is casting a vision of your magnificent future and feeling it in every cell of your body.

Attention is being fully present in the moment. You are aware of your inner life and can see, hear, and feel the world fully. You are conscious of the richness and beauty of *now*.

Intention and attention come together powerfully through time to become the right condition for your vision to manifest. When you *pay attention* through inspired thought, feeling, and action according to your deliberate *intention,* you will *masterfully manifest* what you want.

Question 4: How Will You Know You've Got It?

This question is one of the most valuable planning queries we can ask because it has the person fully consider the plan all the way through the final goal. We ask the person, "If you had it already, what would you have?" This question encourages the development of an evidence procedure that will prove to the person that the goal has been reached.

CHAPTER 8 *The Four Essential Questions in Coaching*

> ***HOW WILL YOU KNOW YOU'VE GOT IT?* Variations**
>
> - When it's totally achieved, how do you recognize you're done?
> - What will be the signals you have reached completion?
> - How do you know when you have completed the project strong?
> - How will you know you have arrived at your goal?
> - How will you know that you are done with this goal?

Careful consideration of the evidence procedure also points out any lack of clarity around the goal itself. As you reach your outcome, you also achieve the deeper value behind the goal. What is the feeling the person is seeking in his or her life? For instance, if a person wants more money, what will tell him or her the goal has been achieved? If the goal was "more money" and the person is given $20, has the goal been achieved? Has the goal behind the goal been achieved? If a person wants "more love," what will tell him or her the goal has been achieved? A hug, a date, a card in the mail, a momentary feeling, a sustained feeling, a marriage proposal? Question 4 allows a much wider range of considerations into the vision and the plan. See Figure 8.2.

137

Art & Science of Coaching: Step-by-Step Coaching

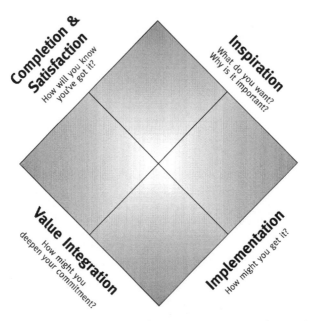

Figure 8.2: The Four Planning Questions in the Quadrant Model.

Using these essential planning questions well requires a perceptual dance between your capacity to maintain rapport, your contracting questions (described in Chapter 7), and the outcome frame described in Chapter 9. These are the four interlaced aspects that create the coaching experience and allow us to fully support our conversational partners as they build strong frameworks for their future success.

You might say that learning coaching is in some ways like learning how to drive a car. First you need to turn on the ignition, warm the engine up, and keep it running through effective rapport. Then we need to do several things at the same time.

We need to aim powerfully with a contracting question to know where we are going. We want to drive joyfully to our intended destination. (Have you ever ended up somewhere you didn't want to be?)

CHAPTER 9

Designing Your Dream: The Outcome Frame

When we create something, we always create it first in a thought form. If we are basically positive in attitude, expecting and envisioning pleasure, satisfaction and happiness, we will attract and create people, situations, and events which conform to our positive expectations.

—Shakti Gawain

The Devil and The Truth

The devil was walking down a road with a companion, and as they walked along they noticed a very excited man under a tree signaling and calling to people in a nearby bazaar. He was holding something and yelling, "Look at what I've found!"

The devil remarked to his companion, "Oh, he's just found the truth!" The companion replied, "That's interesting! I'm surprised that you're not at all alarmed. Something like that could put you out of business right away, could it not?"

The devil laughed and responded, "Oh it's not a problem. He'll turn it into a belief or forget he found it in a day or two!"

A big issue for human beings is choosing to stay truly aligned with our senior truth, our intention beyond every smaller intention, and learn how to keep it alive over time as an important compass for our lives. For example, you may have learned how important it is to "stop and smell the roses" on life's journey, to give plenty of unconditional love and forgiveness to others, to notice the balance points and the give and take that allows you to get engaged effectively in your goals. Yet sometimes we "forget" to live these truths.

Attending to our truthful larger outcomes is not easy when the outside world speaks loudly and one small goal after another challenges the mind. The question is how do we to hold onto the *real* value and remember to live from it in busy and challenging times? Many people easily for-

CHAPTER 9 Designing Your Dream: The Outcome Frame

get their intention or goal when something emerges in their minds that temporarily seem to be of greater importance—lunch, the ringing phone, the urgent meeting, the spilled milk, the late bills, and so on.

Our past priorities can also grab our attention. A person may vow very strongly not to repeat an event that seemed painful, telling himself, "I will never forget that lesson," (Notice the negative framing in this inner message.) He then gets led by the nose with these previous conclusions, spending time and energy looking at the past. Completely new interesting choices may emerge, yet an old priority, useful for a past event, has been made a current priority, so an opportunity to learn, grow, and develop is lost.

This whole symphony of old beliefs and past thoughts can easily distract us from our important goals and aims now. Enter an effective coaching conversation with a coach who is armed with a contracting question (Chapter 6), the four planning questions (Chapter 8), and the outcome frame (described here), and finally we have a support to stay focused on our current priorities linked to what is most important *now*, despite the pull of old distractions.

The outcome frame is an incredibly powerful organizing framework to support transformational conversations, one in which we assist the person to listen to his or her own basic principles for creating a result and not get sidetracked. When you stick with and listen from the outcome principles in this chapter, you will help a person find and focus on his or her core aim even in the midst of strong emotional gremlins. Let's thoroughly explore this frame, which points to four basic necessities for achieving an effective outcome.

What Is the Outcome Frame?

When you, as a coach, ask a contracting question, as described in Chapter 6, the process of outcome listening begins. You take coach position and ask the contract question. To be an effective coach, you need a robust moment of outcome listening, like a conductor's first swing of his baton to get the orchestra's attention. This inner call and focused listening to the outcome frame can start the whole conversation effectively.

Basically, we listen for four main characteristics in the person's reply to the contracting question. If these four things are in place, the person is on the path, on track toward success. If he or she is not, you as the coach will ask questions to begin to get them in place. This acts like a compass so the person can steer and drive toward the goal.

A conversational contract question reminds you to listen actively and ask yourself the following: "Is the person telling me what he or she wants or doesn't want? Is what the person wants within his or her control to do something about? Does the person want a specific, actionable, measurable result (a SMART goal)? Does the person know what will prove that he or she has achieved the outcome?" These elements are the *outcome frame*, and they determine how you will proceed to develop an effective coaching conversation. The outcome frame builds a royal road to successful results whenever it is thoroughly and thoughtfully developed. The characteristics are developed in more detail next.

1. What the person wants from the conversation is *stated in the positive* and is *genuinely important to the person.* To get results, the person must be focused on what he or she wants, rather than what he or she does not want.

2. The outcome for the session is *within the person's control,* and can be maintained by self.

CHAPTER 9 *Designing Your Dream: The Outcome Frame*

3   The goal is SMART: specific, measurable, achievable, realistic/relevant, and timed for completion.

4   Finally, the client has a clear idea of what he or she would like to have at the end of the conversation that proves that this was the very best use of time and energy. The outcome needs to be worthwhile and useful for all concerned. It needs to be *ecological* and fit with the client's whole life according to that person.

Let's go through these one by one to understand their relevance clearly.

Stated in the Positive

To develop a strong outcome, a goal needs to be communicated in positive language.

Effective outcomes always create a positive and inspiring image in mind. Help coaching clients focus on the key questions that create a clear outcome—"What do you want?" "What is most important for you to be, do, or have?" "What is your intention?" "What is your highest vision?"—rather than what they don't want. When visualized, the outcome will always bring to mind an inner movie that makes the person feel good.

For example, "I want to stop smoking" is not stated in the positive. Perhaps the client sees an image of him- or herself with a cigarette attempting to not smoke it, which does not feel good. Support the person to clearly state what they want as a *positive* statement. "I want to make the sustained healthy choice to clean up my system and breathe clearly" is a positive statement that produces a positive inner movie and a good feeling. They visualize themselves living a healthy lifestyle.

When a person states a goal in the negative, he or she is using energy to move away from an undesired state, which feels bad and actually creates more of the negative experience. As we have stated many times, whatever you put your attention on you get more of—what you think about, you bring about. Thoughts become things and energy flows where your attention goes; outcome framing is powerful because you move toward a desired state. An unstoppable outcome or a purposeful intention is something that can be visualized, can be moved toward, and feels good.

When the positive intention is stated, you want to support the person in experiencing the energy that comes from imagining what it will feel like to be, do, and have the result he or she wants. The key is for the client to see himself achieving the outcome and feeling the feelings of having already achieved the goal. Positive feelings help people create and manifest what they want more quickly.

Examine the following coaching examples and check them for the outcome frame criteria of being fully positive with inspired "moving toward" energy. Notice that sometimes we need to listen carefully to the context and tone of voice to notice if what we have is in fact an outcome rather than a hidden agenda or a reversal, holding an inner "I don't want" with an "away from energy" in place.

Example 1: Suppose a person says she wants more creativity, skills, choices, or action steps. A coach can assist her to imagine what these may be and clarify what moves her toward development in each area. We can assist her to unfold and see the "move toward" elements with inspiration.

Example 2: Suppose the client says "I want more protection, security, privacy, willpower, freedom, honesty," and so on. Chances are he or she is probably more focused on "moving away from" concerns. These may include safety issues, addiction issues, self-control issues, interference issues, or inner and outer shaming and blaming issues. These concerns may be still closely linked more to what he or she doesn't want than what he or she does.

When you feel the outcome is lead by an "away from" energy, it is always useful to discuss the higher intention behind wanting more security, privacy, willpower, freedom, honesty, and so on. Basically you are eliciting the outcome beyond the outcome. For example, you might ask, "If you had all the willpower you desire, what will security give you that is even more important?" This helps the person find the true positive intention that is inspiring. This is where a client can really make a visual of his or her true goals.

In the Person's Control

Check to see if the outcome is within the person's control. The best question to ask is, "What do you want that is within your control to do something about?" For example, if the person wants his or her spouse to quit smoking, the outcome is not under his or her control. Likewise, they may not have control over such outcomes as ensuring a promotion, which relies on a combination of inner vision, action, and outer circumstances.

There is sometimes a fine line between an outcome that is under a person's control and one that is not. If a person has a goal of preparing himself for a promotion by looking for a position that uses his best skills or by upgrading his skills to satisfy the criteria for a promotion, or by focusing on becoming the best he can by looking inwardly at this true qualities and attitude, he is moving job creation more into his own realm of control. Even though the final decision is not his to make, focusing on himself and what he can control will increase motivation and confidence.

How to take control of one's own destiny is a question that frequently has many levels and layers, and requires some careful pondering. This is an area where strong coaching creates deep awareness of how much control we really have. The key is for you to assist your client in holding the vision and beginning to explore the details.

You might ask, "As you hold the vision of what you want and feel the feelings of already having achieved it, please reflect honestly: How much of this outcome is within your control? What qualities are you living from as you acknowledge what you control and what you don't? What aspects need to be carefully explored in terms of do-ability? Who else needs to be included? How might you create the best team? Where might you achieve some real leverage?"

Sometimes it may be useful for you or your clients to think of a long line of possibilities, perhaps using a scale ranging from 1 to 10, 1 being "almost totally out of control" and 10 being "almost totally in your control." Your clients or your own projects can all be thoughtfully placed on this line in terms of the dynamics of each aspect's fulfillment. Together you might ask closed questions that support clarity. For example, "Are the decisions of others required to move past gateways? Are the finances still to be obtained? Are some of the timeframe elements still vague and need further specification? Who needs to sign off on the project so it is within your control to take action on?"

Be aware that all "out of control" perceptions tend to pull down motivation and may trigger stalling and confusion. The question is, how might the person take what is perceived as being out of his or her control and bring it into his or her control? What can the person control? How can the person control the thinking in the situation, the attitude he or she holds, the qualities he or she brings to the table, and so on?

For you, the coach, assisting your client to build strong steps toward an actionable outcome means to assist him or her to first list what is in control and what is not. This can really clarify his or her next-step strategies. You might ask, "What knowledge or planning will assist making your project unfold more simply and naturally? What open-ended questions might you ask yourself to build this?"

Exercise: The Two List Method

There is a very effective way to create "in your control" consciousness. We call it the two list method.

- Ask your client to create two lists side by side, one labeled *In My Control* and the other labeled *Out of My Control*. The next step is to brainstorm with your client and ask questions to help the person use big-picture thinking to mentally project forward through the detailed elements of their plan all the way to project completion.
- List in these two columns all information about what is in or out of the person's ability to direct the action. Now your client should have two lists.
- At this point, your coaching conversation begins to explore how to move items from the *Out of My Control* column to the *In My Control* column. This may involve thorough explorations to be able to scale up "in control" step by step around several key areas. These may include action steps and also values, beliefs, attitude, inner strategies, and capabilities.

How can you move this two list conversation forward? You may ask the person to look back from the completion point and visualize some ways he or she moved some *Out of Control* elements from one column to the other. This allows your client to see and feel from the point of future results achieved. This helps develop images or micro-vision movies of the qualities, attitudes, emotional states, beliefs, values, and of course action-oriented steps actually helped him or her reach the achieved goal.

You can also ask scaling questions and get your client to brainstorm possible methods that can be use to move one small step up the scale on difficult aspects of their goal. You might ask, "How might you move one step higher toward workability in this challenging area?"

Is the Goal SMART?

SMART goals are specific, measurable, achievable, realistic/relevant, and timed for completion. Making the goal *specific* targets the goal exactly. When a goal is specific, we know exactly what we want to achieve in the coaching session. Each step that leads toward the goal should be just as specific as the desired outcome.

Each step needs to be as *measurable* and so should the actual goal itself. How do you set an effective measurement for achievement? Each individual step clearly needs to be *achievable* and leading into the achievement of the desired outcome. We need to ask, "Are the steps truly *relevant* and *realistic*? Can success be expected from the actions taken?" If a goal is not truly relevant for the long term in one's life and does not fit with other goals, one may not continue effectively. If the goal is too large, or has too tight a timeline to be realistic, we instinctively know that and don't take the steps to make it happen.

Each step (and the overall goal) needs to be *timed* for completion, with a specific date for achievement. Timeframes are important to accomplishment. We need to assist others and ourselves to respect the timeframe for the goals we put in place and to set them carefully, because we inwardly follow those frames. If we make the timeframe too long, too short, or do not set one at all, the goal easily moves out of our motivation and becomes only a wispy possible choice for the future.

What, then, are the steps to assist our client to make a goal truly SMART?

Inventory the resources the client has or needs to make this outcome a reality. A careful check of needed resources is part of the planning process and naturally starts the person's planning and preparation. Considering the needed resources and how to get them, is the start of progress toward making the desired outcome a reality a good use of time and energy? Ask: Is it *effectively* doable?

Identify specific evidence that will prove the outcome can happen. How will the person be sure his or her outcome has happened when complete? Can the person see the steps? What is the proof that these steps are moving the client toward the goals? Have others done it before?

A statement of outcome that includes evidence of success forms a more powerful vision than a simpler statement of the outcome without evidence. For example, the outcome "I want to have a happier family life" is nonspecific. It can be clarified by adding in the evidence that will prove to the person's satisfaction that he or she is in a happy family situation. Such evidence might be stated as: "I want to have peaceful family dinners five nights a week, with a positive discussion of the day's events. I want one family outing each week. And I want to organize family gatherings on birthdays and holidays." Notice that without careful preexamination and definition, the evidence has no power to compel the attention of the family members or the person. The evidence is specific to each person's interpretation of what a "happy family situation" might mean. Without the evidence, the outcome is conceptual rather than meaningful, tangible, and achievable. By creating an achievable goal, we aim for a specific, measurable, sensory-based result.

A second factor here is contingency planning, carefully exploring the alternatives or Plan B's. If the person sees one way to achieve the outcome, they may be satisfied and will stop looking further for other choices. Listening as a coach, you may want to check for several good ways to achieve the result, such that the person learns to create backup plans that support their direction toward success. "What is your contingency plan? What obstacles might you run into, and how do you solve them in advance?" Plan B alternatives can then be further addressed and clarified through the four planning questions.

Is the Goal Ecological?

Here we step back and examine the big picture. *Ecology* means studying the full range of relevant environmental issues. Evaluating a goal for ecology also means examining whether it fits with other goals and is good for everyone. We may or may not ask these questions, however, it is useful to widen out our attention to the big, big picture at least briefly.

With the client's goal in mind, you might check his or her larger purpose: "What do you want this outcome for?" If the person has difficulty thinking through to their goal at this point, there are two possible ways to quickly resolve their difficulty. First, you may want to request that they consider the higher intention or larger purpose that achieving this goal will create. If the larger purpose is vague and unspecified, you may want to ask questions to have them micro-vision to smaller, more specific and meaningful outcomes. This way, you help them clarify the important aspects to consider as a relevant timeframe for achievement.

Just as an ecologist considers how each part of the environment fits and works together, you will find it relevant to explore how achieving an outcome fits with the other parts of the person's life. An outcome requiring a commitment that clashes with another part of the person's life will not be ecological and is unlikely to succeed. Help them examine all the consequences of achieving the desired outcome as it relates to their whole life.

Sample questions for a coach to ask inwardly:

- In what ways will the achievement of this outcome affect the lives of other people as well as other outcomes the client may have in mind?
- Are there more effective approaches to create mutual benefit? If I can see them as an outsider, has the client considered them? Perhaps the coach may want to start a Chinese menu brainstorming process here. (Remember, the coach needs to refrain from taking on the

energy of being the expert and deciding for the client what is best for him or her.)
- Are there a variety of other and perhaps better sequences to accomplish the outcome or have one outcome assist in completing another? Questioning toward contingency plans and various timeframes might be useful here.
- What might be some better uses of people, time, and energy? Is it worthwhile? How will he know if he has his result?

Valuable Approaches for Developing Futures

As you work with people to help them build a comprehensive plan, the following guidelines can allow a person to leave the coaching conversation strongly empowered by a well-organized and comprehensive inner map of effective next steps.

Dissociated versus Associated Experience

Use *dissociated* visual experiences for planning. You might ask the person: "See yourself and others as if you are viewing everyone on a screen, seeing how the action phase will be developed. When you see yourself in your inner movie and feel the feelings of having accomplished your goal, what steps did you take to achieve the outcome?" This is dissociated visualization, meaning the person is seeing him- or herself on the inner movie screen.

It is important to explore this for yourself because dissociated states have distinctly different qualities than associated states do. A dissociated state means that you are removed from the experience because you are seeing yourself. It is like watching a movie where you see, hear, and feel as if from the outside. You can explore the difference by noticing the quality of dissociation in your own visualization. For example, what is it like if you view yourself riding a roller coaster in your mind's eye? Imagine sitting on a park bench in the amusement park where you can view a separate "you over there" sitting in the coaster car and getting ready to start moving. You can watch the scene comfortably from your seat as you witness yourself flying around the corners, traveling up and down along the track.

In dissociated states, there is always a part of yourself that is aware of another part of yourself having the state, so you have room to design shifts in perception and action. You can remain relaxed and comfortable as you view yourself on this roller coaster. When you view yourself from the outside, you do not deeply experience the genuine thrill of riding the roller coaster, yet you still feel the feelings of the experience.

Use *associated* experiences to build connection. *Associated states* mean linking into full-bodied experience where you are looking out from your own eyes in the vision. For example, explore the same roller coaster looking out from your own eyes while strapped in to the front seat of the roller coaster car. This is an associated experience. You can feel the pushes and pulls, hear the clatter of the roller coaster wheels, see the tracks below, and look straight down the hills.

When we are in an associated state, we are totally engaged in the moment from the inside. All your awareness is captured by what is going on, and due to your total immersion in the moment, you have no attention left over to be aware that you are having the experience.

When people are deeply associative, they gain enormous power when they develop the ability to step out and witness life from coach position. Coach position means designing effective self-observation, witnessing, or watching. This position will assist both yourself and your client.

Coach position, as described in Chapter 1, is the capacity to step outside of an experience to overview all aspects from a larger, solution-focused, dissociated perspective. Only from an effective dissociated

CHAPTER 9 *Designing Your Dream: The Outcome Frame*

coach position can we see the big picture and notice the best questions to ask. Then, when we ask the inner questions, we observe the whole experience. The vantage point allows us to reorganize a workable plan according to our values and the most effective responses to the situation now.

When we make room for and use both the associated and dissociated textures of life, we can ask and test through a wider range of experience. Through stepping in (associating) and stepping out (dissociating) appropriately, we become robust observers. We can step out and notice and ask whether we are living the experience that we want, and then step in to feel the moment with every cell of our body. This is the game of true inner flexibility.

Key Points for Coaching

Other key guidelines for yourself and the people you coach are these:

1 *Always focus on the sensory-rich outcome first.*
   People become inspired and stay motivated when they focus and dwell on seeing, hearing, and feeling the end of a project first. Make sure the person is moving toward what she wants as a completion and that she can visualize the completion in a detailed way with all senses alive.

   When a person is clear on what she wants, be aware that a part of her may likely go immediately into *how*, and the vision may become overwhelming and gremlins may pop up. Therefore, before going into the detailed question of "How will you accomplish this?" spend time on the vision and feel the feelings of already having the outcome. Ask, "Who is impacted by your accomplishment? How are you serving the world through this vision? Who are you being in this vision? What values are you living? How satisfied are you with this outcome? How might you make it even better?" The key is to have the client observe the end result and serve as an apprentice for the future she is moving into.

2   *Bring in the time element.*
"When in the future will I have accomplished this outcome?" A goal is a dream with a deadline. You want the inner movie to be clear, specific, comprehensive, and detailed. A key element is to notice the timing for completion. See, hear, and feel the feelings of having already achieved the outcome on the timeline you want.

3   *Get specific.*
It is often effective to imagine a journey into the future to consider the sensory-based evidence around the specifics of our goals being achieved. The deeper knowing mind is always motivated by specifics. A good example is the goal of the person wanting more money. It could be specified as $500,000 in a savings account at the local bank. The sight of the bank book with the figures entered might be the sensory evidence that the goal has been achieved. Perhaps the goal behind the goal is to find a sense of financial freedom with the comfort of a large cushion of cash. The intangible evidence would be the feeling of safety, security, and freedom. Why are these feelings important? Perhaps the person can access a more loving connection with family and friends and has more time to spend in nature. As the person progresses through the steps toward their

Chapter 9 Designing Your Dream: The Outcome Frame

goal with an inspired state of mind, each step needs its own evidence to show it has been completed satisfactorily.

Consider a map analogy. If you set out to drive to a neighboring city, road signs tell you where you are in relation to your goal. When you define your outcome, your task is to choose your own road signs that tell you if you are on track. What are the achievements you will see, hear, or feel that tell you that you are on track?

4. *Passionately write down the specifics of what you intend to achieve.*

   A study at Yale University pointed out the value of written goals. Writing out goals requires that they are seen first! The Yale University graduating seniors of 1954 were asked if they had set any specific written goals at the time of graduation. Only 3 percent had done so; about 10 percent had specific goals but hadn't committed them to paper. The rest had no specific goals. Twenty years later, they were resurveyed. Guess which group was successful? You guessed it—the 3 percent outperformed the other 97 percent combined.

5. *Implement a daily practice for at least 21 days.*

   To become the person who will manifest the vision, you must implement a daily practice of visioning the outcome as complete. This practice focuses the mind and heart through time. For example, as soon as you wake up in the morning, take a few minutes to focus your mind on your intention and outcome. You might sit in a comfortable position, closing your eyes and visualizing your desires as already being fulfilled. Feel the feelings you would feel if you had already manifested your desire. Radiating the feeling is what creates the magnetism.

6 *Visualize daily in the most effective way.*
For a daily practice to be most effective, a person must be aware of the inner visualization habits. For example, you may have the habit of jumping into your dream and looking from your own eyes associatively. You may even believe the goal will be most motivating if viewed over and over again as associated and happening now. Yet consider that this is only partially true because this form of visioning connects primarily to the emotional-limbic system. (More information is in chapter 2 of Book 1 of the Art & Science of Coaching: *Inner Dynamics.*)

The emotional mind elements of motivation, which are captured by self-talk and auditory internal tone, are alive with associated visualization. This is a good thing! The tone of inner discussion is important, so use a self-motivating tone with your goals. *Say* it the way you want it, as if it is happening now, and feel the feelings of having it. Passionately speak about your future in the present tense with an enthusiastic tone, and write goals down as if they are happening.

For example, "Here I am. It is October and I am so happy and grateful that I can easily jog for two miles and feel energized! I feel magnificent!" As you declare it in the present, see yourself jogging!

This means the visioning is dissociated! See your whole body in action jogging from a camera viewpoint, while making the experience sensory rich.

CHAPTER 9 Designing Your Dream: The Outcome Frame

This is a very important distinction because this way of visualizing connects emotional-limbic and vision-cortex thinking and therefore makes the visioning process much more powerful and inspiring through time.

7   *There are approximately four thinking "chunks" available for our conscious attention moment by moment. Use them well!*
Design your outcome to maximize powerful, magnetizing, streamlined awareness and include enjoyment in all aspects.

This means you may want to help your clients heighten the dissociated, sensory-rich visualizations of their plans with vivid colors and make their inner movies of accomplishment bright, clear, and lucid. You can remind them to see the flow of effective movement, see the parties enjoying the events and moving toward results. Most important: *See* their results and the feelings of having it now! Relish the feelings, hear the motivating inner voice, and see yourself and how your achievement impacts others. Using the inner chunks in this way will maximize the power of the inner movie and create the magnetic effect that draws the parallel to the person!

8   When you are actually doing the activity, be sure to experience and enjoy the moment!
The real time to associate is when you are in full action mode and experiencing real moments in a sensory-rich way. The only way to experience a state is just to step into it and have it! Learn to be in the timeless dimension of now and choose to radiate the feelings of gratitude, joy and love. Choose the thoughts and behaviors in the moment that support you to feel these feelings

now and you will naturally bring more into your life. The key is to be present.

> *The only way to experience a state is just to step into it and have it!*

To summarize and further clarify the associated and dissociated distinction, keep in mind the following items.

- Associated visioning is useful to deepen the feeling and to try on a future outcome from the inside.

- For the most powerful whole brain connection, do your daily visioning process in a dissociated way by seeing your whole body in action. The best inner visioning is done in a dissociated yet sensory-rich manner. This type of visioning is most inspiring through time.

- When you are experiencing a state "now" in the moment of activity, be as fully associated as possible. Focus your thoughts and behaviors in that moment that causes you to feel joy, and associate into the feeling fully. Smell the roses of your life's great experiences now! If you put your attention on the thorns or let your mind wander and miss the moment, you may never experience the magnificence of now.

Often people near the end of their lives notice that they continued to put off enjoyment again and again in their earlier days and missed key experiences. They did this through small inner conversations that required that they postpone satisfaction. Even without reaching the

CHAPTER 9 *Designing Your Dream: The Outcome Frame*

end of one's life, many people talk to themselves this way, for example, "When I finish my thesis then I'll really start enjoying life again." "When the children have left home then we can really begin to live and have fun." "I will enjoy life and be happy when I retire."

9   *Feel gratitude.*
Happiness and pure well-being are full-bodied associative states. Consider whether something is blocking your good feelings in the moment; if so, switching your attention is very important. The quickest doorway to happiness and well-being is to feel the feelings of gratitude. No matter what your situation, there is always something to be grateful for.

Consciously choose to have thanks in your heart and you will automatically feel good. The good news is, the more you focus on what you are grateful for, the more you will pull toward things to be grateful for. You can choose to be happy now, and in doing so you automatically create more of it for your future. What a gift!

Consider inner mantras or affirmations like the following. "I am so deeply grateful for the sort of person I am right now. I am so grateful for who I am becoming. I am so grateful for what I take for granted. I am so grateful for what I am tapped into. I am so grateful that my vision is manifesting right now!"

How will associating into gratitude support you in designing a dream that is even more inspiring? How will gratitude support you in becoming a better coach for others?

What are you grateful for right now?

The following list is a summary of these nine points.

Key Points for Coaching

1. Always focus on the sensory-rich outcome first.

2. Bring in the time element.

3. Get specific.

4. Passionately write down the specifics of what you intend to achieve.

5. Implement a daily practice for at least twenty-one days.

6. Visualize daily in the most effective way.

7. There are approximately four thinking chunks available for our conscious attention, moment by moment. Use them well!

8. When you are actually doing the activity, be sure to experience and enjoy the moment!

9. Feel gratitude.

CHAPTER 10

Inner Alignment with Logical Levels

Open your arms to change, but don't let go of your values.

—The Dalai Lama

Values and Their Design

Values have a design. As we proceed to explore our deep values, we can notice that there is always an inner level of clarity that is recognizable. We can sense this, step into it, and *be* it. Exquisitely, we become what we value.

Value clarity can be explored situation by situation and project by project. This is because values merge and converge and create new convergence designs, much like the formation of a water crystal or a snowflake. There is always a value design implicit in the formations of our natural inner development.

Value Design Forms through Logical Levels Questions

There are many inner choices responding like small identities, inner I's in the personal value design for each of us. These also can be structured, aligned, and clarified to match what is core to our life or to the key projects we organize. We might ask *who* we can become as we take leadership in this life design, both in our own lives and in the lives of those we touch. Logical levels questions as described in this chapter provide a wonderful system for doing exactly this!

A logical levels structure is created with a questioning formulation that allows you to explore, develop, and sense the value and vision connected with any inner structure of value. You can then choose the best structure for in the moment. You can do this wonderful exploration through the logical questions that allow you to sense and see the inner integrity design of your being in your projects. This is the effective work of logical levels questions.

What is truly remarkable in working with logical levels questions is that we can pull out the "value design" in any project, and use this to build your best action steps. If you create clear logical levels questions that allow you to systematize a project, it becomes much easier to compare value with other projects and to choose the best use of your time and energy.

Misaligned Logic in the Success Recipe

As you appreciate the magnificent design of values in the snowflake or crystal, it is also easy to find evidence of misaligned logical levels of thinking and acting in many areas of life. These are assumptions where a small belief system becomes the master of a person's time and energy and disrupts their ability to prioritize well. For example, do you know of anyone who thinks that if they *do* their job well every day, they will *have* what they want, and in turn they will *be* someone important? How about someone that thinks that if they *have* a nice car, they will *be* someone that can attract a loving mate and *do* fun and exciting things?

The transformational coach approach to communication invites you to consider a different methodology to living your best life. Consider that when you first focus on who you are and what you value on the deepest level (how you *are* in the world), and bring your authentic self into how you think, feel, and act (what you *do* in the world), you will naturally *have* the outcomes you want. This is the organization that operates seamlessly and shows a natural, functional inner alignment of the self.

$$\boxed{\text{BE} \rightarrow \text{DO} \rightarrow \text{HAVE}}$$

Logical levels questioning organizes and pulls out these functions, and, as a result, is the coaching tool that serves all the other coaching tools! The benefit you gain in learning how to comfortably use a logical levels approach in various areas of coaching conversations will up-level your coaching communication and your client's inspiration, motivation, vision, and integration. We first describe the logical levels of mind and project organization and then discuss many ways to use this natural inner system in coaching.

Logical Levels of the Mind

What did Einstein mean when he said, "You cannot fix a problem with the same level of thinking that created it"? Robert Dilts, a Californian Neuro-Linguistic Programming specialist proceeding from the earlier work of Gregory Bateson, Bertrand Russell, and Alfred Whitehead, designed an elegant, simple model for observing our thought systems that we now call a logical levels framework. It ties effectively to the neurological levels of the three-brain system discussed in Chapter 2. This simple model is a profound representation of how humans operate in the world.

The logical levels model that we describe here can help you align your environment, behaviors, capabilities, values, identity, and purpose, challenging yourself to consider a higher purpose—be it work-based, family, social, or spiritual—in which you make a contribution outside the day-to-day demands of life. Using this natural inner organization of the questioning approach adds depth to a coaching conversation. It adapts easily to an individual, social, or organizational point of view, and is particularly useful for dealing with change in any of these realms, or in developing effective projects.

In terms of coaching, logical levels, along with the outcome frame, are foundational pieces of a transformational communication structure.

The solution-focused coach approach to transformational conversations uses logical levels as a framework and a process for organizing and gathering information so the coach and client, working together, can pinpoint the best level on which to intervene and explore. We develop precise and useful questions to take those next action steps and make any desired change.

The phrase "logical levels" indicates an internal hierarchy implicit in every project. It shows how each of the internal levels of project development can be progressively more psychologically encompassing and influential than the one below it. This framework allows us to separate actions from results, and capabilities from identity, so that a person can build an effective model of success. Understanding logical levels can help a person move beyond the limiting belief that one's former successes or failures determine one's identity or define one's capabilities. The result is clearer thinking and an increased awareness of unlimited possibilities.

Questions for Transformational Conversations: The Logical Levels Pattern from the Top Down

What, then, are the most effective levels in exploring our project? Visualize a pyramid representing step-like patterns of inner organization (see Figure 10.1). Following Dilts's model, six major integrative logical levels can be seen as central to any project and implicit in any idea. Using a hierarchy, we can describe them from higher to lower:

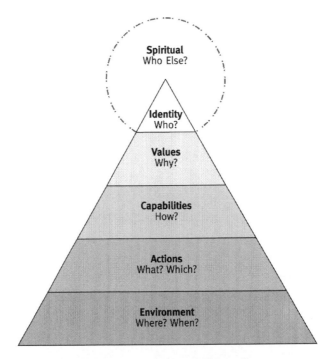

Figure 10.1: The Logical Levels.

Let us look at these levels in terms of aspects of personal life. The **Vision/Spiritual** level at the top refers to the second tier of our lives, well beyond our very personal concerns. It is connected to the questions Who else? Why else? How else?, continuing outward. The *else* word leads second-tier thinking toward legacy and contribution.

Identity, the top of the first tier, starts the *personal* hierarchy of questions. It refers to your basic inner sense of self and your core life metaphors, a key area of listening in any coaching conversation. Identity has primarily to do with intentionally translating your vision and purpose into your mission and the roles you choose to play. This level answers such questions as Who am I? What sort of person am I? What do my life aims say about who I am? What do my choices tell others about this person here?

The **Values** level has to do with your true core values. Values are living concepts felt through the body and perceived as intrinsic to ourselves. They are your inner snowflake or crystal. What are the values you hold as true for yourself and use as a basis for daily action? *Note:* Although values are always positive and ever becoming, beliefs can be empowering, permissive, or limiting. For this reason many people are caught by beliefs that distract them from their important values, such as in the fable of Midas. Many fables and stories with morals speak about realigning toward core values. At the level of values we relate our project to vision, sense of purpose, and the questions of true importance. When we align to key questions of value we ask: Why am I doing this? Why is this really important? What value am I living from? What do I believe is possible? Considering what is most important to me, is it worthwhile?

The **Capabilities** level describes the competencies you currently have and what you are capable of. This level points to your talents, strengths, general skills, and mental strategies that you use and can build in your life. This level answers the question of capability: How can I do this? How do I deal with this? What skills do I have? What skills do I need to build? At this level you use a variety of mental maps, plans, or strategies to generate specific alternatives.

The Action/Behavior level is made up of the specific actions or reactions used in your daily environment. Regardless of your capabilities, behavior describes what you *actually* do every day. It answers questions of specific actions: What am I doing? What actions will get me what I want? What steps do I need to take? What will I do next?

Environment has to do with the external context in which behavior or action occurs. It answers the questions of specific completions: When and where does this behavior occur? When and where will I do this? Today? Next month? Next year?

These levels can be defined and applied with more or less detail, or with somewhat different names and steps. Environment, an external factor, may be included or excluded. Yet the functionality remains the same. The aim is always to differentiate and study the key questions necessary to determine who, why, how, what, where, and when we have the necessary resources to plan for our project.

How Does It Work Operationally?

How do these questions provide such a natural and easy opening into the inner flow of purpose? Your brain works in natural hierarchies or levels of experience. As people visualize using the model, these levels, often hidden in day-to-day life begin to naturally unfold and lead to a flow of visualizations. It is also sometimes helpful to imagine it as a series of Russian nesting dolls, with the higher levels shown in the center and the more obvious action and environment levels moving to the outside like the rings on a tree.

A few examples: Have you ever heard someone talk about responding to things on different levels? Have you ever heard a person say that an experience was negative or challenging on one level but positive or easy on another? This shows that people intuitively have a feel for these internal hierarchies. When you bring the logical level questioning formats and the visual diagram into a transformational conversation, the natural unfolding of the mind is brought into awareness through these logical steps, so that powerful, sustainable work begins to take shape.

This awareness is a huge asset to the client, who by using this framework becomes aware of how changes at one level must be preceded by changes at another level for integral change to happen. This deepening awareness of your own thought processes and the levels inherent within your experience brings higher logical levels into awareness, revealing important aspects that might have remained hidden in the detail focus of everyday life.

The Central "Why" Question: Integrity Organization

Why is this really worth the time and energy to make it central in your coaching? We will soon summarize a list of benefits. To begin, logical levels structures provide a useful visual aid in a coaching session because they help us realign around a natural inner ordering of "importance" that follows these key distinctions.

Logical levels work in a very specific way. The results of the information derived on one level organize and control the information on the level below it. You quickly discover how changing something on a higher level automatically changes information on the lower levels. You learn how to be strategic, because changing something on a lower level may but does not necessarily affect the upper levels.

A person's operations on all logical levels are essential to his or her overall satisfaction and quality of life. For example, making a change in the environment (at the lowest logical level), such as moving into a new home, shifting your living room around, buying a new outfit, eating in a great restaurant, or buying a pet, will *not necessarily* be successful in changing your experience of personal identity (at a much higher level). However, a change at the identity level, such as enhanced esteem and confidence, will likely cascade down through the lower logical levels, developing multiple changes on all of them, including perhaps the kind of home you wish to have, the way you set up your living space, purchasing the pet you wanted, or celebrating by buying an outfit or eating in a nice restaurant.

Another example is to imagine for a moment that you have just welcomed your first child into the family. You've suddenly added "parent" to the list of roles you play (a significant addition to your identity). Now using the model, as you follow the various levels of change outlined, consider for a moment how what you value in life might change with your new child. Maybe a life of adventure isn't as important anymore.

Consider all the ways your new identity might impact the rest of your life. Maybe you are staying at home with your child and accepting that you are awakened several times in the night and need to respond to the pressing needs of the small one. Consider the new skills and capabilities you so quickly need to learn—how to respond to infant messages, how to bathe a newborn, how to be an exceptional parent that supports the wondrous growth and development of your child. As you imagine this new life as a parent, notice that what you do on a daily basis has completely altered due to who you are. As a parent it is clear that your daily activities two months before and two months after the baby's birth are quite different. Consider how the physical environment in which you live would be altered as well—baby toys and accessories, baby-proofing your home, you may have moved, and so on. This example is a demonstration that change on a higher logical level tends to brings shifts to all the levels below it. Shifts on the higher levels have power and control over the lower levels.

As a transformational communicator and coach, you work with people's dreams and challenges. It is interesting to consider on which logical level are the dreams? On which logical level are the challenges? It is essential for you, as coach, to pinpoint these exact levels and know on what level the most effective change could be made. Consider the effects of making changes at that level, and then notice whether true and lasting change could be created if shifts were then made at a higher level.

The Logical Level Benefits

When you work with logical levels, there are significant and fundamental benefits, especially if you show or quickly draw the triangle steps as you discuss with your client.

- **Benefit 1:** The client can use the magnetic pull of the logical levels staircase to discover and rediscover his or her vision as a compelling visual image shorthand to the client's plan. It assists in designing an integral view of the future. The client can easily learn to attend to the future and make it detailed in terms of real-time steps.

- **Benefit 2:** The client can learn how to align his or her vision with values and capabilities as a way to develop the strength to move toward key aims.

- **Benefit 3:** The client can learn to overview key projects, seeing multiple aspects at the same time, linking key aspects from who the client will be as a person doing the project, to why it's worthwhile. The client can point to the important skills needed, and clarify specific necessary learnings or actions to be taken where and by when. This overview allows him or her to build the project in such a way that he or she can find flexible balance between all these aspects.

- **Benefit 4:** The overview function of the logical levels system is wonderful because it allows the client to try on the value and vision of another person involved in the project and thus get a different order of understanding of their contribution that also includes who they are *being* in the project, as well as what they are *doing*.

A good example of this is the story of two very emotionally opposite co-owners of a clothing production empire in the Ukraine who found themselves continually at each other's throats about the best way to build their large and expanding production company. They continually hit conflicts when it came to decisions about next steps with new initiatives. They fought over financial and resource allocations. They seemed to be incapable of seeing each other's point of view.

One partner was an innovator whose inspiration and design ideas had gotten the company productive in the first place. She believed that the timing was ripe for expansion and had some new directions she believed needed quick attention. The second partner was much more conservative but had maintained a productive series of best moves that kept the company strong despite several failed initiatives on the first partner's part.

In doing a careful logical levels vision walk exploration where they walked along markers on the floor representing the levels, each partner was invited to look from the other's criteria and vision. Making physical the steps to Vision and back again, in the other persons shoes they quickly expanded their trust and pride in the other's efforts. Each was able to more fully align with the great value that their partner provided to the enterprise. This assisted them to start much more productive lines of communication than they had known in some years, and to begin to strongly support, rather than undermine each other.

- **Benefit 5:** The ease that a logical levels exploration gives a client in making decisions. As an explorer, you are using the system to compare the personal value of your own use of time and energy as you choose between projects. Logical levels exploration allows you to both sense and see many aspects of the project (especially when associating and feeling all the levels).

By using logical levels you are assisting strong decision making. It is possible to make a strong comparative decision between several good choices, picking the choice that aligns most strongly with your own values and vision. It allows you to work both from inside and outside the various key dimensions of the project. In this way, the client gets very rich data about the core elements.

Using Logical Levels: Coach Benefits

For you, as coach, there are some fundamental and wonderful benefits in using logical levels in your coaching:

- **Benefit 1:** In the first place, logical levels questioning allows you to become a maestro of powerful questions. You move beyond one strong question to a system approach that gives you a comprehensive set of integrative questions that allow for clarity and overview.

- **Benefit 2:** Second, you can assist your client to move beyond blockages and hesitations by asking questions one level up in any area that has become a stumbling block. For example, if the client said, "I don't know what action to take," as coach you might ask, "What sort of person could easily know the next best action? What qualities might he or she have? As you think like this person and take on these qualities now, what might be the next best step?"

- **Benefit 3:** You can learn to use your time and emphasis both to draw a client's attention up to key areas that assist him or her to move to that level and also use the logical levels of every sentence to assist in building the larger meaning tied to the comprehensive overview of his project.

Logical Levels and Organizational Hierarchy

Let's take a moment to appreciate the inner alignment of logical levels in an organization. For example, imagine the structure of a typical large corporation, and notice different groups of people can be usefully thought of as responsible for the overall flow within the company.

- **Vision**: The president/CEO points to the overall vision or purpose of the company.
- **Identity**: The senior management team creates the corporate identity
- **Values**: The finance, personnel, and human resources departments communicate the values frameworks of the organization and assists in defining their importance.
- **Capabilities**: The middle management expresses the capabilities and executes the strategies of the corporation by putting them into action.
- **Actions/Behaviors**: The assembly, quality control, and shipping and receiving departments are responsible for the behaviors the corporation engages in.
- **Environment**: Physical layout and environment is handled by maintenance, security, and custodians.

The actions of the staff at the lowest pay grades and duties—custodian, shippers, factory workers, and secretaries—are *essential* to the operation of the organization, yet these staff members are without power to effect major change at senior levels, such as senior managers and executives. The employees on the lowest levels cannot easily change anything more than their own level of operation.

Compare this to the senior executives, who can create change for all staff members with the stroke of a pen, moving jobs and factories, restructuring salaries—in effect, making massive changes to the levels under them. People making changes at senior levels may not consider the impact of the significant changes that will happen at lower levels of the organization, yet change will inevitably happen.

In this example, note that the administrative support and custodians are essential to a large corporation. This means the lower levels must be considered as essential as the higher levels, it is just that a change on a lower level will not necessarily change a higher level.

Knowledge of the logical levels allows people to steer their lives. The higher levels become the steering wheel as an individual or organization develop vision, purpose, mission, identity, inspiration, choice, and motivation.

Logical Levels: Focus and Outcome Summary

When considering learning and change, explore the following levels to develop and clarify the most important visions. We are engaging our inner vision around our most profound project concerns by developing systematic linked questions about them.

Table 10.1: First Tier of Logical Levels.

Focal point	Logical Level	Outcome Questioning on the Logical Level
Who I Am?	Identity	Authentic Intrinsic Power
My Value System?	Values and Value Criteria Structures for Learning and Development	Inspiration, Motivation and Sustainability
My Capabilities?	Mental Maps and Models, Internal Strategies	Knowledge, Focused Direction and Choice
What I Do?	Specific Action Steps and Behaviors	Definite Inspired Actions
My Environment?	External Context	Locations, Opportunities and Overcoming Challenges

This first tier of logical levels deals with the *person*. Generally speaking, identity and values are the most important here, because these levels determine how you hold your deepest sense of commitment to who you are and what you offer. Your values inspire your identity and awaken your deepest commitment. As you progress down the logical levels, your commitment to each succeeding level may tend to lessen. Change is easy to make at the level of environment, where you are least committed and least resistant to change. As we have shared, moving your bed to the other corner of the room or eating at a new restaurant are not too challenging for most of us because a change at this level has little or no impact on the levels above it. Lasting change is created when the higher levels commit to a new vision, identity, or value system.

Also notice, it is possible to have rapport at some levels, but not at others. Generally speaking, the further you go up the levels, the greater the degree of rapport you can achieve. Mismatching at a higher level is liable to break rapport that has been established at a lower level.

The second tier of logical levels can be explored above the level of identity, and assists one to focus on who else is impacted by choices made. In the second tier we begin to move from just "I" to "We". These levels assist a person to explore and enter into the design of spirituality, legacy, the grand vision, or connection to a greater whole. The higher logical levels on the second tier focus on the larger contribution, for example, to family groups, professions, societies, language groups, cultures, and the planet. It is sometimes useful to physicalize the diagram as the two complementary tiers. Our clients sometimes gain strong insight by visualizing through the second tier of contribution as they consider their project or even their life. We can draw it reversed on top like a small hourglass to show its power:

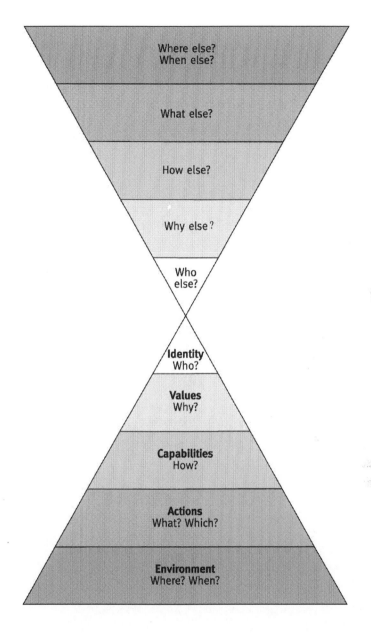

Figure 10.2: Second Tier of Logical Levels

Logical levels questions can also be useful occasionally if explored from the bottom of the triangle upward. This is sometimes helpful when defining an outcome to yourself or to someone you are coaching. If the client's focus is "I want to create a life I love, but have no idea what I really want," the coach might ask the following questions that start at the bottom of logical levels and work upward.

- Just suppose you started to have a life you love, what sort of environment would you create? What sort of surroundings would you see, hear, and feel?
- What actions might you take on a daily basis?
- What skills and capabilities might you demonstrate or share with the world?
- What attitudes and beliefs might you want to adopt (or live from)?
- What sort of person might you want to be?
- Who else might be affected by you being this sort of person? And who else?

By leading this person through the logical levels from the bottom up, the client will determine what the desired outcome is, bringing new clarity and vision to the outcome.

Behavior and Identity Confusion

As a coaching framework, it is important to notice if and when a person is confusing logical levels as they focus on a task. The most important one is the confusion between behavior and identity.

Have you ever heard yourself or someone else say, "I am so stupid for doing that!" Or have you ever heard someone say to a child, "You are a bad girl!" when the child has done something wrong? Notice these are examples of identity statements (top level) made about an action (much lower level). Many people walk around thinking that people *are* what they *do* and judge themselves and others accordingly.

You are not your behavior, and neither is anyone else! Who you are is a possibility much larger than anything you have ever done. At the identity level, you are neither your behaviors nor the result of your behaviors.

*You are not your behavior
and neither is anyone else!*

Transformational communicators support people and themselves to separate their actions from who they are. The confusion that exists when you conflate *who you are* with your *environment* or *behavior* prevents you from seeing yourself as essentially whole, complete, and unbroken. People experiencing this confusion tend to engage in self-blame (if the behavior or environment is not what they would have preferred) or egotistical thinking (if they have been blessed with a prosperous environment that encourages a behavior). In either case, the person benefits when he or she is able to separate behavior from identity. When the loop between behavior and identity is severed and the vicious circle no longer exists, an empowering new mental map is created that is self-fulfilling, rather than self-defeating.

For example, a person living in poverty may believe their environment created their behaviors that makes them who they are as their identity today. With the focus on environment and behaviors as a dictator of identity, integral change is impossible. Yet when the identity is separated from behaviors and environment, change immediately becomes possible at the higher level of identity. This change will affect beliefs and the expression of values, which will affect capabilities. This, then, naturally creates behaviors and ultimately cascades down to affect environment.

Imagine the power of leading clients, through their own thought process, to this realization—that they are not their behaviors and environment and never have been. When expressed as logic, many people will not be able to internalize this shift. When led by matching logical levels and leading the client to the next higher level and considering their solution from there, integral change is easily accomplished and accepted.

Coaching Conversations that Use Logical Levels with the Outcome Frame

Transformational conversations powerfully weave together all aspects of the person's reality with outcome-oriented questions and logical level questions. Including logical levels questions with the outcome frame questions results in a powerful synergy. Just as adding a bass section enhances the lead guitar, bringing greater resonance and range of expression to the overall musical texture.

The span or timeframe focus for transformational communication is set by the outcome frame. We address how to get from here (present state) to there (desired state). Our coaching will then be enriched and deepened with logical levels questions. Adding depth to the outcome frame with logical levels enhances a person's understanding and commitment toward achieving a goal. It has them stand tall as the big H. (see Figure 10.3).

CHAPTER 10 *Inner Alignment with Logical Levels*

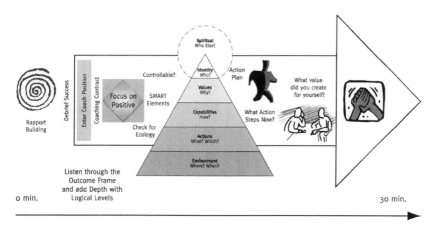

Figure 10.3: Logical Levels with the Outcome Frame

By starting with the outcome frame question "What do you want?" and then moving into "How might you get what you want?," you help the person assess his or her outcome from a logical levels perspective. The following coaching session worksheet provides a series of questions that can bring the depth of logical levels to the coaching conversation.

In the coaching session questionnaire that follows, note the use of open-ended questions, within the outcome frame itself; the use of SMART goals, and the weaving in of logical levels to help the person form a complete vision of the desired outcome at a deep, integrated level, far beyond the surface level of asking "What do you want?" Even though this is only a worksheet, take a moment to practice and to note the depth and richness of the structure of these questions in a coaching conversation. You can test its capacity to promote change, especially when combined with deep rapport and an ongoing respect for the person's model of the world.

Before using the worksheet as a basic structure for a transformational conversation, we encourage you to use the following exercise for yourself, to see, hear, and feel the difference it makes to add logical levels into the outcome frame.

181

The Logical Level Coaching Worksheet

We have ___ minutes together, what might be the best result you will get from our time together? (Listen for desire being stated in the positive, and within his or her control. Am I clear on what the person wants to have by the end of the session?)

How might you get what you want? (Use a logical levels unfolding to answer this question. Listen for SMART goals.)

Vision Who Benefits?	
Identity Who do you want to be? Who are you when? What sort of person would you be?	
Values Why is this important? What values does it develop?	
Capabilities How will you achieve it? What skills do you have? What skills do you need to develop?	
Actions/Behaviors What actions need to be taken? What steps could you take to support X?	
Environment Where will you want this? When will you do it?	

How might you make this more meaningful? How might you deepen your commitment? How might you take this further? How might you move past any obstacle? (Listen for deepening, contingency planning/risk management, check for ecology.)

How would you know if you got it? (Listen for an evidence procedure and tracking toward it—if you had it already, what would you have? What is your evidence that you are on track?)

Audio Exercise: Structural Listening

You will find this exercise similar to the one about global listening. In this case, as you listen, or simply reflect, consider how the emphasis on the words is added information about the logical level the person is using at the moment.

Listen for emphasis: "*I* choose to finish writing the article today." The emphasis on "I" tipped you off that the inner processing I was using was focused on the identity level.

How about, "I *choose* to finish writing the article today." Compare that to "I choose to *finish* writing the article today." "Choosing" indicates a focus on the values level you choose. The emphasis on "finish" is a capability, a skill, and hence indicates the person is operating from the logical level of capability.

"I choose to finish *writing* the article today." This indicates the focus is on the logical level of actions. "I choose to finish writing the article *today*." That would indicate the person is operating from the level of environment.

Your response could be chosen to build rapport by responding on the same level as shown by the client. You may also choose to build rapport and enhance a transformational conversation by leading the client from that level to the next higher one to effect change more quickly and easily.

Suppose you have a client who has difficulty finishing what he starts, blaming the environment for his own lack of follow-through. Suppose the statement made to you was "I *choose* to finish writing the article today." You might respond: "Wonderful! Who you *are* is the kind of person who will find a way to get this done! *You choose* to do it!"

By solidifying the use of the word "choose" with your own emphasis, you enhance rapport. By inviting the person to consider this choice as part of who he is, you lead the client as they begin internalizing the knowledge that he or she is capable of making the choice. It now becomes more and more part of his identity. For clients who have difficulty completing what they have started, it is a powerful assist in building their vision of themselves, being the one who chooses to finish.

Listen again, and practice for yourself. Which level is someone communicating on with each of the following statements? How might you respond, on the same logical level and to lead the client to the next higher?

- I am always excited to *start* things.
- I am always excited to start *things*.
- I *am* always excited to start things.
- I am *always* excited to start things.
- I am always *excited* to start things.

Write some sentences for yourself, and practice!

CHAPTER 11

Amazing Grace: Taking Action and Completing the Conversation

We are here to witness creation and to abet it. . . . We are here to bring to consciousness the beauty and power that are all around us, and to praise the people who are here with us.

—Annie Dillard, *Pilgrim at Tinkers Creek*

The River Crossing

I have done many long walks on various trails along the Pacific in my lifetime, and the one that had the most impact on my life was the very first journey.

As a young woman in need of some solitary time, I left my children with family and arranged a seven-day hike along a very difficult Canadian trail on the west coast of Vancouver Island. I prepared well with a very light pack, maps, compass, and a brand new tide table, as advised.

Having traveled the trail for three days, I discovered that it was tough slogging with many steep climbs, ladders, and knee-deep mud in some places. Although this trail followed the Pacific Ocean, it only really approached it at the river mouths and campsites. Sore and tired by the third day, I sat eating my breakfast and contemplating the beach. The tide was far out with multiple gulls searching around the rocks for food.

Looking at my map, I noticed the next campsite was only ten miles away. Feeling my sore muscles, I wished for a short day. I noticed that the flat, straight route by the sea made the campsite seem much closer. "Gosh," I thought, "I should be able to walk there by the shore in four hours maximum." Hopeful, I checked the tide table and noted that the tide would not be in for six hours to come. "Done!" I said to myself. "I'm heading out, and I will walk along the shore to the next site."

I found myself walking beside a high, concave cliff with a flat stone base, much like the cliffs of Dover. It was magnificent.

For two and a half hours, I enjoyed the hike, breathing the fresh air into my lungs. I was walking primarily on flat rock shore and was able to explore many deep water-filled pits containing small beautiful tidepools filled with colorful sea anemones and other amazing creatures. I

Chapter 11 Amazing Grace: Taking Action and Completing the Conversation

paused often to enjoy them. There were also large crevices or fissures in the rock floor, where it was necessary to climb down three steps and up again on the other side. I noticed there was not even one place available to climb uphill and leave the beach. All connections to upper trails were blocked off by the huge cliff face.

About three and a half hours into the remarkable hike I suddenly realized that quite a bit of water was now filling the crevices. Shocked, I checked the tide table. It didn't make sense to me to see all this water starting to appear. Reading the tide table more carefully, I realized I had made a huge mistake. The numbers on the tide table I had read in the morning were actually for high tide. In about three hours the spot where I was standing would be under at least 8 feet of water. I was in trouble. And it was too late to go back. I had to move full speed ahead.

Starting to run down the beach, I entered my longest hour in this lifetime. Each time I jumped the crevices, they were filled with rushing water. Some were very wide, almost impassable. I realized after one very scary jump that I could not go back and might meet an impassable gorge ahead. It was slippery and very dangerous. I moved as fast as I could, but the water was coming in quickly. There was no place to climb.

I began to see pictures of my funeral, my children now orphans. I began to pray fervently: "If I survive this, my life will be of service," I promised the world. "Is it possible, please, to have this life?"

It was a long hour. The water rose quickly and was flowing quickly across the plane, getting closer to the cliff wall with each wave.

Far ahead I could see where the cliff curved out toward the sea. "Maybe that's the river mouth," I thought. "I'm sure, if I move as quickly as I can, I will get there before the water gets me." And I did. It was a huge effort.

I was sloshing as I arrived, but I climbed the small rocks at the end of the short peninsula in about a half an hour. The band of curved stone was very low, about five feet. Eagerly, I peered across to the other side.

It was indeed the river, but not what I expected. I had been told to expect a river with a crossing. What I saw was a large river mouth flooded with the incoming tide. No crossing was possible in the fierce riptide. To my dismay, I also saw that the cliff face continued up the river mouth for at least 200 yards, ending in a deep gorge. Moving up, beyond, or across seemed completely impossible because of the swirling river itself. Far across on the other side, half a mile away, I saw some tents.

Painstakingly, I edged sixty feet up the river mouth until I could go no further. It was impossible to climb, but ten feet above me were some gnarled tree branches from a tree coming out of higher parts of the cliff. I was blocked in all directions, and the water was rising.

All of a sudden, I saw a man emerge with dishes from a far-off tent. He began to walk toward his side of the river. It seemed like he saw me. He put the dishes down and went back to the tent. I didn't know if he wanted to help me, was ignoring me, or even if he could see my plight or not. I continued to pray, hoping against all odds that he wanted to help me. A few very long minutes passed. It seemed like over an hour.

He emerged from the tent with another man, and they were both carrying ropes. They were hurrying toward me now, and even though the water continued to rise, I knew I had help.

The next part of this story is one of the most spectacular events I have witnessed in my lifetime. Hardly looking at me, the man with the rope eyed the tree branches ten feet above my head, a long way from him across the river. Carefully making a lasso, like in the old cowboy movies, he twirled it above his head and threw with all his might. It was a perfect throw over a vast space and caught the broken tree branch exactly. There was now a rope across the swirling river. The water continued to surge, and I watched in amazement.

With the other rope, he made a second lasso and after several efforts to get it to me, I was able to catch it. Shouting, he told me how to tie it around my waist. Now there were two ropes: a guide rope to hold, and one holding me. With the two ropes I dared step into the heaving river. I was pulled off my feet immediately, but I held on, regaining some footing. I moved slowly, step by step, over the rolling rocks with freezing cold water swirling to my neck. At times I lost my footing; however, with the help of the rope and the encouraging words of the men, I was able to cross.

The two men took no time to help me out of the water and introduce themselves. When they saw I was safe, they scolded me. One ran back and loaned me a paper blanket. I fell asleep in minutes. They were packed up and gone before I awoke.

Since that experience, crossing the river of life has seemed like the heart of my vocation. We all have a river to cross in our lives—a situation where circumstances demand courage and vision. If we cross it, our life opens forward into an even more profound journey. If we don't, we metaphorically drown in the hopelessness and helplessness of our current situation.

The difficulties may easily sweep us off our feet. Yet if we trust that support is available if we request it, and hold firm to our purpose, we can find the passageway into our next level of living!

The rope we hold on to, to guide us, is our values. We must declare them, tie them on knowing they are anchored well, and have them guide us to the far shore. With our values linking us to our vision and to each other, we will dare to step out.

When we dare to step out into the chasm of real inner leadership and genuine trust, we will cross the river, into the future of our dreams.

The Language of Taking Action

Coaching conversations become productive when they lead to effective action steps that implement the learning or discoveries made in the session. After a person has explored a goal visually and has imagined the details of completion, the most natural move is toward determining specific steps to undertake the plan. Once the steps are effectively visualized as clear, concise action items, seen well from several points of view, and linked to what is most important to the client, the person is on track to reaching the goals with power, grace, and full satisfaction.

At the point when a conversation shifts from exploring and testing to deciding on specific actions, a linguistic framework can be powerfully created to support the application of the plan. People usually get the results that they decisively choose and do what they strongly declare. This is a critical point in the coaching conversation. Your language as coach needs to shift from the soft, open-ended exploration mode of checking alternatives to decisive motivation words and tones that support clear choices and definitive plans that will be completed. Let's discuss this in detail.

Total Session Progression: Open-Ended to Closed

When you are at the beginning of a coaching conversation, you ask exploration questions that invite the person to look for his or her most valuable choices. In this early phase of the conversation, you use open-ended questions and curious, soft language. You are supporting the person in visualizing exactly what he or she wants and to wonder about the specific potential directions and steps needed to get there. Softened language when visualizing choices helps a person to relax, stay open, imagine best plans, think through timelines, add examples, and discover various plan B opportunities.

To keep a coaching session solution-focused, encourage the powerful visioning and feeling of the end result, and then support the person to micro-vision the key details of the steps, especially the challenging areas in their action plan. To micro-vision means to identify and visualize the more challenging details of the action plan until the steps become clear and the client has methods for accomplishment in mind. Remember, all things happen first in mind, then in reality.

As the action pictures become clarified, the session sharpens focus onto specific action steps. The person may do this him- or herself, or the coach may lead with action questions that assist the person to begin to formulate his or her first commitments in a key area.

Notice the qualities of such questions.

- Considering our work today, and your short- and long-term goals, what actions are you willing to commit to this week?
- What do you commit to accomplish this week to solidify the learning from our conversation?
- What, then, are your specific action steps?

- Notice that these are closed questions. Other closed questions or statements may be used where appropriate to direct the person to focus on his or her outcome and how to achieve that outcome by designing solid action steps.
- Are you 100 percent committed to doing this?
- So you *will* get this done? When?
- So you are *deciding* to do this?
- So you are clear you're really *doing* this now?
- *Can* you accomplish this? *Will* you do this?
- Got it! You *are* going to *make this happen,* correct?
- Are you saying you *will* take action tomorrow?
- Okay, you're *choosing* plan A and going for it. Is that correct? What will your action steps *be* this week?
- Are you saying, "I am choosing to do this now!"?
- You're committed, it's clear. Would you please summarize your time line and *what specifically you're going to produce* in the next seven days until we talk again?
- *You are* talking action then! Exactly what *will* you accomplish?
- So you are saying "Yes!" to taking action, correct?
- You said you touch the sacred "yes" within you. Are you *completely willing* to say a complete "Yes!" to doing this starting today?

You will notice that the timed and closed action questions serve a distinct and important purpose. With a carefully place closed question, a person can declare a strong yes or no and then organize accordingly. A strong yes sparks commitment, determination, and a clear focus to continue progress toward a goal, whereas a no response is an opportunity to uncover a more powerful aim. Making use of closed questions for this purpose helps a client deeply recognize his or her inner agreement toward achievement.

The Tone of Action Language: The Turn in the Conversation

Everything shifts as the client orients and commits toward specific action steps. The client is now negotiating with him- or herself and assessing best plans. When turning a session toward a committed plan, the coach can assist this negotiation by holding the frame of action and using an action rhythm and tone. The wizard tone (see Chapter 5) calls for strategic action. It is often useful to emphasize energy as well as upbeat rhythm. This adds power to the client's action focus.

As he or she takes the plunge into the commitment to produce a specific result, you, the coach, can use your voice to strongly support the client's own inner voice and vision to get into action. We also often help when we encourage several visual rehearsals of steps, so that through the visioning process the person gradually increases the realness of their inner videos of the specific actions they will do.

Action Language That Compels

When people explore options at the beginning of a coaching conversation, a coach can assist when they use softeners and open-ended questions, including words like *might*, *want*, *may*, *could*, or *possible*. Soft, open-ended language makes exploration easy. For example, the question "What might be some of the ways to start to do this?" is a softer and more open-ended question than "What will you do to achieve this goal?"

Toward the end of the session, it is useful to catch and play back the person's own strong action words and their strong action nuances. At the point where people have discovered specific choices or best opportunities, the tone of the conversation must change. At the key moments where people begin to determine and select specific action steps, it is useful to make your own tone strong and decisive, and begin to use *their* words for certainty of results leading to inspired implementation and completion. You can do this by backtracking or you can request that the client backtrack. Both ways have power for a person, and the key is to be sure the person's action words are honored. These words may vary from person to person.

Action words are always a very personal system used and understood as a personal code. They differ from culture to culture. For example, some people take clear action when they use necessity phrases like "I must," "I should," or "I have to." Others are more likely to use possibility words like "I will," "I choose," "I can," "I decide," "I'd love to," or "I am." That means that if you, as coach, try out their words that seems to inspire and empower them, repeating them their way, you help them take action powerfully. You also produce the experience of strong coach support. The key is to listen closely to the words that energize the client and not to use the words they use that tend to deflate their engagement.

Many people may use phrases like: "I *should* get this done," but the should doesn't lead to empowered action at all. Another word like "I will risk this then", or "Okay, I'm *doing* it!" does get their inner action pictures moving with brightness and life.

If his empowered action words are *choose* or *can,* or simply *do* (as in, "I am *doing* this!") then use his words right back to him. For example, "What do you choose to do?" "So can you do this then?" "Are you doing it?" If the empowering word is *choose* said in a particular decisive tone, use that in your question: "Are you *choosing* to make this happen?" In other words, as a person moves to the action phase of the coaching con-

Chapter 11 Amazing Grace: Taking Action and Completing the Conversation

versation, simply ask questions about the next steps using the most powerful action words phrased in his or her own tonality.

As coach, ask yourself about the words you notice that assist each specific person in jumping off their own inner diving board of life and into strong action mode around a challenging goal. What gets them into the water effectively? Each individual is different. Does he move with passion and enthusiasm when he says "I *will* do it." At this point in the conversation you assist strongly if you ask, "So, *will* you do it?"

The key is to listen closely to the verbal expression and how it is said. Does the client say:

- Love to?
- Choose to?
- Decide to?
- Desire to?
- Want to?
- Need to?
- Ought to?
- Have to?

Are the words said with an inspired empowered tone of choice? Or are they said with a desperate tone, like there is an oppressive force outside of them making them do something? If you are not sure, ask the person to scale his or her motivation level from 1 to 10. Check if there is a stronger inner phrase that gets his or her inspiration and motivation battery really charged.

In summary, the key to using the most effective action-oriented language so the person steps up and takes action is to listen closely to the words that seem to inspire and motivate the client and use *those exact words* with him or her.

Alternative Approaches if the Action Plan is Delayed

If the exploration component of your session is drawing to a close without a clear plan, it is important for you, the coach, to support the action plan birthing process. Any action steps are better than none. For a very abstract goal (50,000 feet), or a goal that needs further exploration, inquiry, research, or observational sub-goals are useful. Clearly, taking observational or information-gathering steps are valuable action steps to help shape the client's best plan and are the first steps toward finishing the plan.

This is also where we may encourage some stepping-stone tasks. Anything that has the person consider multiple avenues for effective achievement and the capability to move full speed ahead by trying out a even few steps is very empowering. Most people have become stuck by considering only one choice or some kind of polar opposite. Consider that in some ways we are like midwives, and every birth is different. Sometimes the birth happens after a long labor, sometimes short, sometimes easy, or sometimes very hard. We work with the person, step by step, as they engage their way.

As the coaching session draws to a close, to encourage this birthing process you may offer curiosity questions that stimulate the person's deeper knowing system to suggest some specific action steps. Scaling can assist this process.

- What are three small action steps that you could take that will move your plan forward this week? What could you commit to?

- If there were a few key action steps that could move this from a 6 to a 7 this week, what might they be? Will you do them?

- So what actions are you considering doing to really get this moving? Could you begin with something small?

CHAPTER 11 *Amazing Grace: Taking Action and Completing the Conversation*

- To explore this vision, what steps could you begin with, even just to test it?

- How could you move strongly to get this going now? What are three ways?

- What are the most important prioritized action steps you can do this week to make that happen?

Chinese menu selections are useful if the person remains stalled, and often get the pictures moving again. For instance, you might say, "Some people might research the new skills at the library, some might go and talk with someone in the field, some might explore with video, or observe the key details that intrigue, or find another way to move this ahead? What do you think?"

Approaching Closure: The Where and the When

The coaching session is moving to a close. Energy in the voice stimulates the juices of action. If the person seems to be lingering in thought, we may want to remind him or her in an upbeat way: "We only have about five minutes left now, are we on track here?" This reminds them of their own commitment to take action, and often engages their awareness of the power in the renewal they are promising.

One last step for you as the coach is to repeat the person's timeline for clear confirmation or to have the person declare specific steps with timeline back to you. This timeline confirmation with the client, spoken as a commitment, brings this last important part of the session to a close with the strongest possible support system in place, both from him or her, and from you, the coach. Learn to repeat:

> **Coach**: "So you are saying this *will* be done by Wednesday morning, then?"
>
> **Client**: "That is what I am saying, alright!"

As we ask the person to complete we also check for completion: Has the conversation been as productive as possible? Is the person empowered?

As coaches, our total aim in finishing the session is to help the person:

- visualize exactly what he or she wants and sense the power of really having this happen;
- step out of the vision and see through time by explore alternatives and micro-visioning various alternative steps on how to achieve the outcome;
- imaginatively try on and test the best steps until they are clear what will work best getting what he or she wants;
- clearly define and enthusiastically declare to themselves their SMART action steps and see themselves at least one more time actually taking those steps;
- "just do it" after the coaching session; and
- learn and grow from the feedback they get after taking action.

Final Footprints: Debriefing the Value of the Conversation

After a client determines his or her actions or tasks, we are nearly done. There are only a few key elements left to support the client in making the commitment real.

CHAPTER 11 *Amazing Grace: Taking Action and Completing the Conversation*

A powerful first step is for the client to debrief and declare the value of the session, and hear (and feel) him or herself acknowledge that value. For this purpose it is highly relevant to ask the client at the end of a session: "What value did you create for yourself in this conversation?"

Other examples:

- "What did you learn about yourself today?"
- "What wins did you create in this session?"

This question gives the client room to step into true satisfaction by honoring and acknowledging the work he or she has done. The client recognizes and debriefs the progress made within the conversation.

This is not self-serving; it keeps the focus on the person and her development. Her own self-esteem is increased as she acknowledges herself for playing a big game. Self-acknowledgment means that a person cleanly and clearly completes a strong conversation. By truly considering what an outcome means to each person and what it will take to achieve it, a client affirms self-respect.

When questions are voiced in this way, the value of the person's progress is acknowledged, appreciated, deepened, and enriched. These questions provide an opportunity for the person to declare value and commitment, reaffirm value, and create real satisfaction. This is also an opportunity to listen deeply and globally to the person, sensing his or her commitment and growth through time, and becoming aware of his or her future fulfillment as if your own. Enjoy them.

The Final Acknowledgment by the Coach

It makes a powerful difference to complete the coaching conversation with a strong final acknowledgment from you as coach. It is wonderful to finish with a few words sharing what you see in the person, lighting on those aspects you know as a springboard to his or her development. By completing this way, you will sense the bond that has begun to form between you and the client. You have shared a special experience together, and this is your opportunity to cherish the work he or she has done. In the last few moments of the conversation, express your response to his or her commitment and who you see the person becoming as he or she lives the action steps that will lead to the dream.

Enter this final part of the conversation by stepping out of coach position and genuinely acknowledge and appreciate the client. This added degree of a more personal presence supports a powerful conclusion.

Your aim in this one to two minutes is to keep your focus on the client and communicate what was important and special in being present for the session. Be careful not to evaluate the session or his or her specific choices, even positively, because this would put you once again in the role of the expert.

What stood out for you globally as you witnessed the session? What was the pleasure in experiencing the client at work? How did you experience and enjoy the stretch toward long-term value? Can you be expressive? You may want to emphasize his or her natural capacities and obvious strengths of motivation to complete what he or she has started.

Some people close with as simple an acknowledgment as a heartfelt "thank you!" said with presence. Others say a few words from the heart to speed the client's journey. You will find the best way for you to declare the power of what you have witnessed.

Exercise: The Logical Levels Acknowledgment

A great way to complete a powerful conversation with true attention to all the qualities just mentioned is to use what we call a logical levels acknowledgment.

This simple process emphasizes some of the distinctions and choice systems key to a person's life.

- The top level of thinking might be called Identity: How does the person discuss who he or she is?

- The next level is called value-added. What are the most important values touched on in the session?

- A third level is the level of capabilities. How did the person discuss his or her capabilities and moving them further?

- A fourth level are the action steps chosen.

- A fifth might point to his or her specific plans for their use—where and when.

- At the end of the session you can use these natural logical levels of commitment to honor a person by touching at least three of the levels as you acknowledge him or her. You can often do this in one powerful sentence to complete your session. The process is timeless in the way that all acknowledgments are timeless. Moreover, this type of acknowledgment allows for authentic appreciation to be powerfully expressed.

To become effective with this, you will want to practice on your own. To discover how the process works, it is easiest to start with the following small exercise.

The Exercise

It is often easier to begin this exercise by thinking of some people you really care about. This gives you a good opportunity to practice, and then later you can move the process out to your clients and others. With a bit of practice, you can use it in the key final moment of a coaching conversation. It relies on connecting to your own deep knowing about personal unfolding for yourself and for others.

Find a quiet spot where you can speak out loud. For practice, find photos of your loved ones preferably taken with yourself in the picture. Or, simply allow yourself to visualize them in your mind's eye. Think about this person you love in terms of his or her finest and most enduring qualities.

Also visualize a logical levels triangle (refer to Figure 10.1). It is easy to learn to visualize the simple triangular logical levels form, and then in your mind's eye place it like a translucent frame in front of the individual you want to acknowledge (see Figure 11.1).

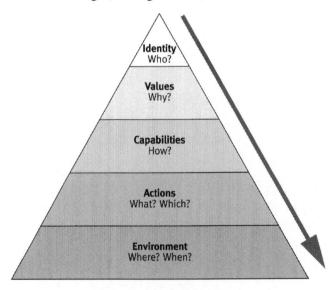

Figure 11.1: Logical Levels.

CHAPTER 11 *Amazing Grace: Taking Action and Completing the Conversation*

Imaginatively, hang the levels on a pretend hook in front of the person and simply start speaking to the person, making appreciative statements from the top down. You will find that moving, top down, from one level to the next will flow naturally when you put your attention on simply honoring the person. These are what we call logical level statements because, like a waterfall, each naturally flows down to the level below it, creating a wonderful flow of acknowledgment.

Here are some examples to build your skills of this form of acknowledgment. Follow the logical levels structure from the top down at least to the action level as you speak. For example, experience this one-sentence acknowledgment from an actual coaching session:

1. [*Identity*]: "Wow! I really enjoyed working with you today. Who you are is a powerhouse of real determination,

2. [*Value*]: and you are so clear about what is important to you,

3. [*Capability*]: and you go for it in a "no-holds-barred" way,

4. [*Action*]: so that you are finding remarkable ways to move past all obstacles that face you

5. [*Environment*]: and your aim is clearly producing results in the community and in the world. Terrific!"

This is easier than it seems at first, because the logical levels shape the natural form of the acknowledgment in an authentic way. All you consciously need to do is to intend to find something genuine and inspiring about the person on each level. (Later, for your clients in a session, you will acknowledge the person for what you saw in the session.)

Now, pretend to address this special person either vocally, mentally, or on paper. Practice it in various ways, and explore doing it vocally just as the thoughts come to mind. Use all the levels shown in the example and the next outline. Express appreciation on each level, beginning from the top of the logical levels and moving step by step downward through each. Be sincere, and communicate in a way that backtracks and supports what the person sees as his or her strongest commitments and values. Share with the value you perceive in the person and the power within to reach his or her vision. Recognize who he or she is *being* in the world.

An easy way to do this is to finish the sentences as I have started them here, either vocally or by writing them down.

1. Who you are is . . .
   (Example, myself to a loved one): "Who you are is a courageous and farsighted human being."

2. And, it is important because . . .
   (Continued with loved one): "It is important because it is wonderful to see the value you are creating for those around you . . ." (Alternatively, you could express "And the value of who you are is . . .")

3. How you have been developing these capabilities . . .
   (Continuing with loved one): "It is exciting to watch you develop all the flexible capabilities you are now showing."

4. What actions you are taking . . .
   (Continuing with loved one): "And the actions that you are now taking really make a difference! I see how you are moving in a deliberate way, with strong committed steps."

5. Where and when you take them . . .
   (Continuing with loved one): "As you continue to joyfully step up and take action, I am grateful to have the opportunity to watch the results unfold. What a pleasure!"

CHAPTER 11 *Amazing Grace: Taking Action and Completing the Conversation*

Here is a summary of some effective practice steps.

- Visualize a transparent logical levels diagram in front of the person you wish to acknowledge.

- Notice what is heroic and exceptional in this person's way of being in the world.

- Use the starter thoughts *who, why, how, what, where* and *when*, as shown, to get your own creative juices flowing.

- Begin at the top of the logical levels diagram and finish all the sentences, focusing on and briefly speaking to the person's finest qualities. Allow your deeper knowledge system to strongly finish each sentence at each level.

- As you speak, truly feel the respect, honor, and affection that you have for this individual, and allow this respect to inform your voice tone and nuance. Basically, you share from the heart and allow your authentic voice to carry the message. You will feel natural and at ease.

- Once you begin sharing, start with who you are at the top of the logical levels triangle and select your sentence completions quickly and easily, moving at least down to the action level.

- Enjoy the person thoroughly as you speak.

As a coach, your personal contribution to help others awaken the genius within themselves and to help them commit strongly to their life and their own development. When you use a logical levels acknowledgment like this at the end of a coaching session, a powerful championing and recognizing supports and strengthens the person's commitment to achieving the outcome. This is your opportunity to add wind to your clients' sails and speed them along the path to their dreams with amazing grace.

CHAPTER 12

The Self-Examined Communicator

All of life is education and everybody is a teacher and everybody is forever a pupil.

—Abraham Maslow

Beyond a World of Criticism: Go to the Light

In the early 1950s at a convention of physicians in New York City, Dr. Milton Erickson planned to do a very standard demonstration of hypnosis features useful to doctors. Because the convention took place at a medical hospital, the coordinators asked him to find a nurse in the hospital who would be willing to be the demonstration subject. Looking through the halls, Milton met a young nurse named Laura, and after a brief conversation, she agreed to be the subject.

The demonstration was planned for the afternoon. During the lunch hour, Milton remarked to the organizers that the demonstration subject would be a young nurse named Laura. "You can't use her!" they all exclaimed. "Her friends have told us that she is suicidal. She is planning to quit work in two days and says she plans to end her life. Her friends are very worried about her, as are we. If you use her as a demonstration subject, this could make it worse." Milton thought about this for a moment and responded, "I suspect otherwise. She is excited about this now. If I don't use her as a demonstration subject, she is far more likely to have a negative response."

When the afternoon program began, Laura proved to be a willing subject. Milton was able to show the hypnosis features he had planned for his demonstration very quickly. With time to spare, he then asked Laura about some of her favorite places in New York City. She answered, "The botanical gardens, the zoo, and Coney Island."

"Then let us take a small tour," said Milton.

Inviting Laura to do a detailed visualization, he had her inwardly tour some of her favorite pathways in the botanical gardens. With pleasure, she described a path with multicolored dahlias and purple forget-me-nots, banks of flowers of different sizes and shapes. She *continued describing many areas of the gorgeous gardens, marveling at the trees from around the world, including the tiny bonsai.*

Next, Milton took Laura to the zoo, where she enjoyed visualizing the different kinds of animals from various continents and how strange some of them were. She mentioned the baby ones, and Milton had her linger to watch a young monkey with her newborn, and then a baby rhinoceros, shyly peeking out from behind the legs of his protective mother.

Finally, Milton took Laura on a tour of the harbor, where, through her visualization, she walked past all the cargo ships docking and unloading. Finally she went out to Coney Island, where she observed picnicking families, children making sand castles on the beach, and young lovers strolling along the waterfront.

When he was finished, Milton thanked Laura, said goodbye, and left. One week later he received a phone call in his Arizona home. "Laura has disappeared!" said the organizers of the conference. People had gone to her home and found the apartment completely empty. She was an orphan with no family, and they had no leads as to where she might have gone. Based on her former declarations they believed she might now be dead. "And you may have killed her!" they added.

"Oh, I'm sure she will show up," said Milton.

One month later, still no sign of Laura.

One year later, still no sign of Laura. At the physicians conference, Milton was shunned.

Three years later, there was still no sign of Laura. Milton continued to be treated as dishonorable.

Six years later, still no sign of Laura. Now the topic was completely closed, people had forgotten about her. But not Milton.

Twelve years later, Milton received a phone call at his home, and a woman's voice on the other end of the line said: "You probably won't remember me, but my name is Laura, and I was your demonstration subject twelve years ago at a conference of physicians in New York City."

"Oh, I remember you well, Laura," said Milton, "Where have you been?"

"I have just returned from Australia, where I live with my family, a husband and three children," she said. "After your demonstration twelve years ago, I was very moved and happy and I went for a walk along the harbor. I talked with a young officer from a freighter that was the leaving the next day for Australia, and he mentioned they badly needed a nurse aboard. I was leaving my job and on the spur of the moment decided to go with them. I gathered my passport and the things I needed and left. On board I met my future husband, and we started our new life in Australia. I'm here for a short visit, talked with an old friend, and she mentioned I should call you."

"I knew you were okay," said Milton. "It's great to have something be completed well!"

What would Milton's experience be like for you? Many people would visualize the worst. They would be distraught with self blame, misgivings, and the fear of criticism. This story leads to an important topic—the critical role that self-doubt or self-confidence can play for all of us.

When people questioned him about Laura, Milton always declared he was sure that she was fine. His confidence, trust, and deeper knowing guided his response. He never seemed to doubt that she was okay.

If there was criticism, anger, and fear-based thinking from people who are your colleagues and mentors, and it was kept up over many years, how would you respond? Would you still maintain inner certainty, clarity, and trust that the highest good was revealing itself? With Milton, there were twelve years with no sign of Laura, and still, he maintained calm assurance and trust that somewhere in the world she was okay.

The Nature of Self-Trust: Aligning with Your Vision and Your Mission

Being a transformational communicator means being congruent and aligned with the coaching process and the coaching techniques we have shared so far in this book. When coaching others, it is of prime importance to come from a clear, clean coach position where you do not project your model of the world, even as you live by it. If you are not self aware or self-managed, you might unconsciously listen at level 1, the level of personal opinion, and transfer your preferences and judgments onto the person with whom you are connecting. You are not even aware that you are doing it.

For transformational communicators, it is imperative to acknowledge that *who you are for others* is only as powerful as *who you are for yourself*. With this in mind, it is very important to have integrity with the tools and processes you use with others. The way to demonstrate this integrity includes living by example and "walking your talk."

The easiest ways to develop the skills described in this book are to learn to demonstrate the power of transformational communication in your own life. You can do this through self-reflection, development of a daily meditation and visioning practice, and by hiring your own coach so that you keep using and developing the coaching tools and distinctions in your own life.

Strong solution-focused coaches have an aligned purpose, a value-based vision, and an operative mission that reflects who they are and what they contribute. Ask and scale yourself on the following questions.

- How self-aware am I? How clear am I becoming about what I want?
- How much am I using effective self-evaluation and self-appreciation?
- How much am I open to receiving and integrating the best of other people's feedback?
- How much am I reframing things that happen in my own life so I can learn, grow, and evolve?
- How can I begin to visualize what I genuinely want to be attracting into my life?
- How could I start to widen my awareness of that intention being fulfilled?
- How can I start to move my awareness to how enormously blessed I am, and start to feel some of that gratitude right now?

Take the necessary time to develop your own inner alignment and self-clarity. Self-doubt is dissolved when you openly go inside yourself and answer these questions.

- What is seeking to emerge now in my life?
- What is my unique purpose?
- What is my vision that is based on my deepest values?
- What is my mission that reflects who I am and what I contribute?

Consider that your vision, values, and mission based on your unique contribution powerfully determine the way that you see the world and will move you far beyond your inner gremlins or fears. When you are self-examined and have consciously chosen with a clear intention to live your life on purpose, the next step is to focus on becoming the right condition for the vision to manifest. The self-questions develop into the following.

- Who am I becoming for this vision to manifest?
- What is my growing edge? Where are my opportunities to grow and evolve?
- What areas need my attention?
- What can I let go of? What will I step into?

As you answer your own questions you will clearly get your Hu-man assignment relevant to the moment. This is the essence of self-coaching. Once you are clear on who you are to become and what your assignment is, the next step is to be completely willing to say a complete "Yes!" to doing your inner work. When you sincerely take on the self-directed Hu-man assignment and you know your true inner direction and work, you can relax into the vision you want to manifest in your developing life.

The key is complete willingness do what ever you need to do to be the *walking environment* of your value-based vision and mission now! Through your self-examination and self-responsibility you will follow Gandhi's great message and "be the change you want to see in the world."

Human Complexity and Dynamic Emergence

Ask and you shall receive. Give and you shall receive beyond all asking.

—Michael Beckwith, *Inspirations from the Heart*

The complex, dynamic, and magnificent Hu-man game is to play with and off of one another for the purpose of coming up with our own creative ideas. Transformational communication based in the coach approach supports this dynamic emergence on individual and collective levels.

As expressed throughout this book, the coaching conversation honors each unique individual expression as perfect by accepting without judgment the vision, values, and mission that make up a person's purpose. When coach and client are able to be with one another in this space of wholeness, deep rapport, trust, and intimacy are built. Most people seldom have the opportunity to be listened to in such an honoring, respectful, and empowering way. Such a space of unconditional appreciation allows the energy of creating miracles.

Awakened Awareness, Self-Knowledge, and Listening

We each have a unique set of approaches and filtering systems that judge and give meaning to the world around us. These assessments, feelings, preferences, opinions, suggestions, and other inner strategies guide our personal decision making. If we are not aware of our unique ways of thinking and mindful of how they can impact other's intention and actions, it is possible to negatively influence people.

The common phrase "I don't understand where you're coming from" is an indication that you are listening only at level 1, your own personal opinion, and not respecting another's world view. Such misunderstandings rarely happen when you take the time to do your own inner work, perhaps using some of the various coaching processes described in this book or getting your own coach, so you can stand firmly in your inner alignment and honor another through the power of coach position.

With awakened awareness and self-knowledge, we are capable of cleanly and clearly holding the space for other people by meeting them exactly where they are and powerfully being a champion for their desired change—not what we want for them or what we perceive to be the best way. People feel heard, honored, and understood when you acknowledge and respect the viewpoint created by their unique model of the world.

Beyond Bias: The Advantage of Allowing

> *Each person's map of the world is as unique as their thumbprint. There are no two people alike . . . no two people who understand the same sentence the same way. . . . So, in dealing with people try not to fit them to your concept of what they should be.*
>
> —Milton Erickson

The advantage of honoring difference and allowing people to come up with their own unique solutions is that they will take responsibility, be accountable, learn on a deeper level, and show up more powerfully to reach their aim. Plus, their inner discovery and chosen path will match their unique desires more effectively than any outsider-provided solutions.

The intention is to allow people the opportunity to come up with their own answers. When we keep personal bias out of the conversation, we support clients in developing strategies, approaches, and victories that are entirely their own. This is true empowerment.

Advancing Your Skill Development Through Time

Highly effective transformational communicators bring the following attributes to a conversation by using the coach approach.

- Attentiveness, comfort, and caring
- A relaxed neutral state that honors, respects, and accepts clients just as they are
- Honor of the person's model of the world and a knowingness that the person has all the resources within to be a success
- Support and consistency that champions the client and expands the client's best efforts
- Commitment to establish clear agreements and keep promises
- Outcome-oriented questions, asked with real curiosity
- Focused, contextual, and global listening used with consistency
- Comfort with silence to allow the person to go deeper
- Flexibility and trust of intuition while tracking toward the outcome
- Commitment to maintaining an approach that honors the person's agenda

As you work with the skills in this book and take time to reflect and explore whether you understand a person's use of language, physical space, and different perspectives, you will raise the level of genius in the person with whom you are connecting. Through your conversations together, the person will start to use high-level solution-focused thinking as a practice of choice. They will streamline inner visioning strategies, clarify their values, become the condition to manifest their vision, and live from their commitments.

The rapport and trust will be deepened as each of you learns the power and intimacy of transformational conversations. In turn, you will both deepen your capacity for trusting relationships overall.

Consider that, even if you have been coaching or receiving for years, a transformational conversation is always useful in further awakening the genius within. Relationship and transformational communication is a two-way street. You get as much as you give.

Aligning with Vision: The Use of Overlap Language

A person's perceptual space is theirs alone, and transformational communicators learn to deeply respect it. Recognizing that this space is an important part of a person's experience adds a further dimension to a transformational conversation. When a coaching session is done in person, rather than over the phone—for example, by sitting next to a person, instead of in front of him or her—you allow people to use the space directly in front of them as a "drawing board" on which to create their vision. By sitting to their side, you give them more space to see the movie of their best future play right before them. The person gets to direct his or her own inner movie of the most perfect outcome.

At the same time, the hierarchy is removed and you encourage a sense of togetherness and inclusiveness that together "we" are working toward the outcome the person wants. The drawing board, blank canvas, or movie screen is the open space in front, and we are allies sitting side by side, working together in the deliberate creation process.

Over the phone we can still assist the inner visual drawing board to be a focus point by moving people's attention gently to their vision when it is appropriate. This can be elegantly done by using simple overlap language. To overlap means simply to move from words or feelings first expressed to a vision. We simply link the two with a question. Here are some examples:

- John, as you *think* about these alternatives, what specific steps do you *see* yourself taking?
- Mary, as you notice how you *feel* about this move you are making, what do you *see* as some good actions to accomplish the result you want as quickly and comfortably as possible?
- Michael, I appreciate your perspective on the software roll-out. As you notice what you are *saying* and what you have *heard* the others share, what do you *envision* as the best methods for the transition?
- If you, Sam, were to zoom in on some detailed pictures what do you notice are the key details that you want to make sure will happen? As you think of these actions, take a moment and step in briefly. As you notice this, do you feel the way that you want to feel in this situation?

The overlapping approach allows people to create rich representations of experiences that they wish to have. It allows them to start visualizing effectively in those areas where they need rich action maps. Short videos with sound, where we can also imaginatively step in and feel the results, offer us well-planned, sensory-based perspectives and move us forward with certainty and positive expectations.

A Picture Can Speak More than 1000 Words

Using drawings or other visual tools also encourages each person to move toward a vision and the power of visualization. The cerebral cortex is responsible for the planning function of the brain, and it has thousands of times more processing power than the emotional brain. In fact, many of the processes in this book are designed to encourage the flow of visualization.

Using images and imagery encourages people's deeper knowledge systems to bring information to the conscious mind. The coach approach adds to and helps people gain insightful ways to access their deeper knowing. We give people natural access points to inner awareness that might otherwise never be brought forward.

When you ask questions and create visual diagrams that invite multiple perspectives or different perceptual positions, you are able to explore different options—and, in a sense, try on different hats. Changing perceptual positions, imaginatively looking from the eyes of other people or from an overview position can be extremely useful in supporting people to evaluate key options and test perspectives.

Just as when you climb a mountain the view changes at each new level, excellent questions invite new ways to view the world. With each advancing step you become aware of pathways you could not see when you were on other parts of the mountain. With these enhanced possibilities now visible, you see more ways you can move beyond old challenges and gremlins. With each level, you add increased mastery to your skills. You learn and experience the integral change available through transformational coaching.

Integrating the Science of Inner Processing

What the caterpillar calls the end of the world, the master calls a butterfly.

—Richard Bach, *Illusions*

As you continue your development and training as a transformational communicator, you will continue to build flexible skill sets based on a deeper understanding of human neurology and the science of effective inner processing. With these skills you will be able to assist the development of creative flow states of seeing, hearing, and feeling that powerfully support and contribute to people's deeper awareness, breakthroughs, and genuine transformation.

Just as the conductor of an orchestra leads the different sections and instrument groupings into forming great music together, so will you lead people to integrate their separate pictures, feelings, and sounds of a specific result into a satisfying coherent whole. As they feel the lifting feelings that come with the images, they become the conductor and weave the inner musical ensembles together into a flowing series of actions that work as a whole—the whole of their lives.

As you naturally and fluently build rapport, use open-ended questions and other solution-focused tools such as overlap, and as you easily listen from coach position, effectively use outcome frames, and develop the steps of a strong coaching framework, you will orchestrate amazing results together. You can engage in the processing that weaves the structure of the client's original focus with a structure of powerful coaching frameworks. Working together, you help the client vision, explore, and think in profound ways. This inner work will lead, guide, and direct them to do the things that will create the outer reality. In this way, people achieve fully and take responsibility for their own magnificent creation.

Transformational coaching is dynamic spiritual camaraderie based in sacred service. As you choose to live this level of service, your questions will form seamless invisible support, like the cocoon in which the person gradually builds their transformational potential and lives in reality. Then you watch them fly with the beautiful wings that are theirs to unfold.

CHAPTER 13

Overview of Transformational Conversations Using the Solution-Focused Coach Approach

This chapter offers a basic summary of the elements of an effective and complete transformational coaching session followed by examples of session transcripts.

Estimated time for the following steps: 20–45 minutes.

Rapport Building Elements

- Connect with the person, create a warm atmosphere.
- Match tone, pitch, speed, volume.
- Use verbal softeners and backtracking.

Contract (Session Topic/Focus)

- What do you want to accomplish in this 30 (45, 60) minutes? What would be the very best use of your time?
- Person describes challenges. Person focuses on aims, values, commitments, and passions.
- If necessary, shift toward customer from complainer/visitor.
- Use motivational words, reframe as required.

Coach Explores Outcome Planning Steps and Questions

- What do you want? Why is this important to you?
- How will you get it? What is your contingency plan?
- How might you commit to this long term? How might you really be sure to make this happen? How might you take it further? What commitments needed?
- How will you know if you've got it?

Coach listens at Level 2 and 3 for Outcome Frame Responses

- Positive?
- Within person's control?
- SMART goals
  (**S**pecific, **M**easurable, **A**chievable, **R**ealistic/relevant, **T**imed)?
- Contingency plan?
- Ecological? (Fits with all other goals of the person)

Fieldwork and Design of Effective Actions

- Considering our work today, and your short- and long-term goals, what actions are you willing to commit to this week?
- What will you do this week to accomplish your outcome?

  Note: We have just five minutes now until our session will end (five-minute warning).

Person Asked to Debrief How the Session Was Most Useful to Them

- What was the value of this session for you? What are your wins from this session?

Coach Completes by Acknowledging and Sharing Heartfelt Appreciation for Client

We encourage you to use these steps for a general coaching checklist from time to time.

Following are two solution-focused session transcripts that show the elements of a session in action. It is useful to notice the elements as they appear sequentially.

Coaching Session I

A 15-Minute Coaching Session with Lucy

Coach: What would be the best use of the next 15 minutes?

Client: The first thing I want to concentrate on is a plan for a healthier life.

Coach: We have 15 minutes today. What would be the key part you most want to get a result with where you could use these 15 minutes to make it happen?

Client: First it must be my inner *discipline*—that's what I need to strengthen!

Coach: So, for you right now, discipline is the key area that will support a healthier lifestyle?

Client: Yes, discipline is the key!

Client: Lucy, I am curious, how do you know when you *are* disciplined?

CHAPTER 13 *Overview of Transformational Conversations Using the Solution-Focused Coach Approach*

[Note that the coach does not know what discipline means for Lucy and does not want to make assumptions. She starts very gently to explore the meaning of the word for her client. She also noticed that Lucy was making a face when saying the word *discipline* and is checking that this is a positive outcome with toward, rather than away from energy.]

Client: If I was disciplined, I would be eating healthy five times a day, each a healthy small meal, exercising twice a week, swimming once a week. Even though I'm doing it, mostly, I have to *force* myself to do it. I don't like to cook healthy meals five times a day.

Coach: Since you said you *are* doing it now, what do you want to achieve in the session that gets you what you want?

Client: To find motivators to do it regularly. I want to really build in the habits that inspire me, rather than forcing myself.

Coach: Where on a scale from 1 to 10, would you place yourself now, if 10 is real sustained motivation and discipline, and 1 is scattered and forced discipline?

Client: I'm about 5.

Coach: So, where do you want to be on this scale by the end of our time together?

Client: At least a 7.

Coach: Okay, how might you begin to move this number up?

Client: This is the real question! I want more motivation.

Coach: Would it be okay if I ask which of the things that you are doing now gives you the most motivation?

Client: The exercise!

Coach: Okay! You are enjoying the exercise! I hear a change in your tone. Where are you on the motivation scale now, Lucy?

Client: I have moved up the motivation scale. Exercise feels good.

Coach: So you *are* really motivated to do it?

Client: Oh yes, once I'm there I'm fine, but to take all my things, go out the door . . . that's hard. It's about getting there. That is the hard part for me.

Coach: Okay, just suppose you could assist yourself here. Some people might find ways to exercise where they don't need to travel. Some people might exercise with a friend, or they discover what gives them the most pleasure and do that, or they get multiple ways to exercise to keep it interesting, or they build the travel into key areas of their weekly schedule. What are some of the ways you could increase your motivation and discipline?

[Client shows a strong body response here. Her face flushes and she becomes very energetic, speaks fast, and even laughs. This question, said in a flat, off-hand manner, is called a Chinese menu question because it lists several alternative choices. Choices are expressed without attachment and tonality, the coach asks the client for even more alternatives. These types of alternatives are described more extensively in Chapter 5.]

Client: Well, I have done a lot already. I've found a fitness center, a young and handsome trainer, and I get a great massage after exercise. That is all working except the timing. [Tone changes to excitement.] Oh, I have a new idea! The best would be to change the exercise time to mornings so I don't have time for excuses. Why didn't I think of this

CHAPTER 13 *Overview of Transformational Conversations Using the Solution-Focused Coach Approach*

before? This is a good idea. I'm getting close to making it work!

Coach: So you are deciding that this one key action will make a difference. One action—going in the morning—will increase your motivation?

Client: Yes, this one adjustment increases my motivation.

Coach: Okay, let's keep going. What else?

Client: I need to repack my backpack every night so I don't have to do it before I leave. Well, I think that will do it! I need to really make sure I get everything for my backpack in the evening. I'll set that up with a checklist before bed tonight.

Coach: We are almost to the end of our time together. Would you simply say again what your new plans are for this week?

Client: It's really simple, and it will make all the difference. I'll pack my bag in the evening and put it by the door. I'll set my alarm, then get up and go. I will start with two or three times a week, and add more as I get better.

Coach: So when will you start?

Client: This week! This is such a simple idea. I am glad I thought of it because I'm sure it will work. Yes I will do it!

Coach: So where are you now with your discipline question?

[The coach holds out the client's scale on a piece of paper marked at 5. The client takes her pen and moves the mark to 8 with a flourish.]

Coach: Wow, you have moved past your original goal! We are at our close here. What was the value of this session for you?

Client: It was so easy. I love easy! Talking about it had me discover I'm much farther ahead than I thought. It helped me see the solution. In each session I move forward, more and more. My plan is good and will bring me satisfaction. I can see clearly what to do and this helps me for the next steps that will follow next week.

Coach: Watching your exercise enjoyment is a pleasure for me. You are truly committed to your health and are growing new habits in a powerful way. It is fun to watch your enthusiasm turn into capabilities.

Coaching Session II

A 25-Minute Coaching Session with Emma

Coach: So here we are, and we both have the time and space to have an amazing conversation. So, if the next 25 minutes was to truly be of service to you, Emma, and it produced the highest and best result for you in your life, what might that result be?

Client: I guess for me, helping me try and find ways to have more flow and grace in my life. I do have those periods in my life when things are in balance, but they're not as frequent as I would like them to be. So how do I get in touch with that, or what can I do to make that happen more often so I do feel like I have more balance in my life? Does that make sense?

Coach: Yes it does. I'm curious, I wonder if you mind me asking, if you were to ask yourself a question that if you asked it and had it answered would truly transform this area of your life, what would be the question that you would want to have answered?

CHAPTER 13 *Overview of Transformational Conversations Using the Solution-Focused Coach Approach*

Client: The question would be, what's stopping me? Because I know it's all about me getting in my own way. It's not about other people; it's about what I'm doing with my life.

Coach: I'm going to give this back to you. I'm going to invite you to notice on a scale from 1 to 10, 1 is "you know that is very preliminary version of the question" and 10 is "you know that if you had that question answered it would truly transform your life." So, your question is right now, "what's really stopping me?" How would you rate that question?

Client: [long pause] I'd probably only give it a 7.

Coach: If we were to play an even bigger game and ask an even more valuable question for you, to move it up just a little tiny bit, what's the new question that will be of *even better* service for you?

Client: I want to say, "Where am I going with my life?" But I don't know where that came from. Hmmm. [long pause]

Coach: So again, I'm going to invite you to go within and tune into the part of you that knows that you know, that you know on the deepest level. I'm going to read this question back and just scale it again on a scale from 1 to 10. So, the new question is "Where am I going in my life?"

Client: [long pause] Honestly that question is only a 5.

Coach: Okay, tune back into that part of you that knows that you know, that you know. If you were to find that part of you in your body, where does it reside in your body right now?

Client: Hmmm... I think it is in my gut.

Coach: Welcome this part of you and just as if this part of you could speak and tell the whole truth, ask this part of you "What is the question that if I had it answered, would truly

229

transform my life and allow for balance to be natural and easy for me?" [long pause] Just listen to what it says.

Client: I think I've lost touch with my vision or my dream. I think I'm too caught up in doing the task and the . . . I've lost touch with what I really want to be doing or . . . I used to do a lot more community work and a lot of . . . I seem to be pulling in, but I seem to be busier and doing more tasks, like I'm going around in circles or something. I think it's about looking at where I want to be going at this point in my life. I feel like I'm in a transition period.

Coach: So as you hear yourself say all of this, I'm inviting your gut to speak now from the place of knowing that you know, that you know. What's that 10 out of 10 question that will best support you now? [long pause]

Coach: What are you noticing, Emma?

Client: My mind is jumping all over the place, so I'm not listening to my gut anymore. [laughing]

Coach: As you naturally and easily quiet the mind, go back into your gut and listen to your gut. What might that question be?

Client: I feel my gut, but I can't hear the question.

Coach: Let's throw out some ideas for your gut to consider. Is the question, "What sort of person do I need to be to live my vision? What is *really* my vision? What is my mission in this next phase? Who am I and where am I really going? What's my passionate purpose? [long pause]

Coach: And as your gut "steps off of" the questions, what's an even better question for you now?

Client: My gut says, "How do I reconnect with my passion and purpose?" [long pause]

CHAPTER 13 *Overview of Transformational Conversations Using the Solution-Focused Coach Approach*

Coach: How do I reconnect with my passion and purpose?

Client: Yes! That's it! You see, I know I'm on a path, but I'm floundering in it a little bit in my life, so, how do I get back on the path?

Coach: How do I reconnect with my purpose and get back on the path? How would you scale that question?

Client: That is good. It is at least a 9.

Coach: So, for you right now is 9 a strong enough of a question to move on for right now?

Client: Yes, I think so. *How do I reconnect with my purpose and get back on the path?* I actually feel some energy around that. I can sense a quickening and some excitement. This is it.

Coach: Emma, do you have a capability of having another chair nearby you?

Client: Yes. I have to go into another room.

Coach: Okay, you can do that, or you can do this standing or you could even do it on a piece of paper, so whatever for you feels like it would be of the best service. Whatever you choose, go ahead and create the space right now where we're going to have the capability of shifting perspectives.

Client: I'll stand up.

Coach: Okay, great. As you're standing up right now, I want you to notice that there's a space beside you that you'll have the capability to step into. So if you're standing up, I want you to tune into this question right now, and if you think of this question again, go ahead and state it out loud for yourself.

Client: How can I get back on my path and continue the journey that I'm . . . continue the life that I'm meant to be

231

living? *How do I reconnect with my purpose and get back on the path?*

Coach: As you hear the question, tune into the part of you that for whatever reason seems to be getting in the way of you already having that question answered. [long pause] Where do you find it in your body?

Client: My head.

Coach: And as you tune into your head and notice that as the block, ask your head, "What is your positive intention for me right now?"

Client: It says "safety." It wants to keep me safe. That's the first thing that comes up.

Coach: Just ask your head, "If you were to keep me safe in all the ways you want fully, what is it that you want through keeping me safe that's even more important?"

Client: What's come up for me is that perhaps if I change, then other people in my life will not be very thrilled when I . . . the people that depend on me and people that are close to me in my life, something about relationships being affected and . . . [long pause]

Coach: So this part wants relationship? If this part was to support you in having relationship in all the ways that you want fully, what does it want through supporting relationship that's even more important?

Client: It says "love."

Coach: As you vibrate with love right now, thank that part of you. [pause] Emma, would you be willing to play a little game with me?

Client: Sure.

Coach: As you stand vibrating at the level of love, I'm going to invite you to imagine you've gone to bed. Its night and you've gone to bed and you're having a great sleep. . . . I mean this is just a sleep of all sleeps, your system is fully nourished and in the middle of the night something really special happens—in fact, a miracle happens. It's an amazing miracle, and you've been able to answer this question, *"How do I reconnect with my purpose and get back on the path?"* You've been able to answer it naturally and easily as you vibrate with love. And, as you vibrate with love, you know that there's nothing in the way and tomorrow you wake up thinking and feeling completely different. Take a moment to think of this thoughtfully and vividly for yourself right now. Just notice all the thoughts and beliefs, the states of mind that have created this miracle, this transformation within you. When you feel this miracle in every single cell of your body, let me know.

Client: Yep, yep.

Coach: And now Emma, open your eyes, and take a step into that other space you created beside you. This space represents the day after the miracle. Let me know when you're there.

Client: Yep, I'm here.

Coach: Now, just suppose it was indeed the day after a miracle and you had this question answered and you were vibrating with love fully, how would you know?

Client: Well, the sun's shining [laughing] and full of energy. I'm phoning people and actually I'm gathering people together and I'm inviting people that are closest to me to come and I'm going to cook for them, I love to cook, and I love to have people, close gatherings, and I'm going to share with people what my dream is and how this is important to me and to all of this. I'm going to ask them for their support.

Coach: So, as you notice yourself doing that now . . .

Client: Oh, I feel like crying. Sorry . . .

Coach: Please, take your time. [long pause]

Client: This feels so right. [pause] Yep, okay, I am ready.

Coach: So, as you see yourself gathering this group, sharing how important your dream is . . . [pause] What do you notice about the tone of your voice?

Client: Oh, my voice is strong! I'm speaking quickly, and I'm passionate in my way. I'm speaking and my excitement's coming through my voice when I'm talking.

Coach: What do you notice about the vibration in the room?

Client: Oh, there's lots of energy in the room. It's a lot of . . . the room is humming, there's lots of . . . yeah, lots of love, it feels good.

Coach: What do you notice about your grace and flow?

Client: I'm completely in grace and flowing . . .

Coach: How do you know you are in grace and flow?

Client: I don't feel any stress or tension; I'm calm. Usually when I'm out of flow with life and lack grace, I get very stressed and have very short fuse. I get headaches.

Coach: As you see yourself living in this graceful, flowing way, what are you doing differently now that you're sustaining a way of being?

Client: I am sharing more of who I am. I'm involving people in my dream.

Coach: As you see this you in technicolor with a full panoramic size picture [client laughs], on a scale from 1 to 10 how satisfied are you with that as the future you're moving into now?

Client: Oh, it is definitely a 10.

Coach: Emma, we've got about three minutes left in our session. As you notice yourself owning this fully and you notice yourself naturally and easily sustaining this way of life today . . . one month from today, two months, one year, two years, five years, all the way through to the end of time, how do you sustain this grace, flow, and love to live your dream and share with others?

Client: Well, I see that each step I take, I see the energy growing and the colors getting more vibrant, and I see everybody winning, like it's a rather than people resenting me spending time building this dream, everybody's also part of this and benefiting.

Coach: As you notice that vibration carrying all the way through the rest of your days, again notice how you naturally and easily sustain this for yourself, no matter what comes up. And as you think of the three things that you might do now to sustain this, what are those three things?

Client: Well, first I'm going to go camping tomorrow with my husband so I'm going to tell him. I mean, I've talked to him before about it, but I haven't really shared my dream in this way with him. Second, I will add this vision to my meditation in the morning before I go out the door. I want to relive this and put a plan in place to bring all those people together that I want to share with.

Coach: Emma, how confident are you that you will follow through on these actions for yourself?

Client: Well, honestly . . . [long pause] I'm pretty good about talking myself out of things.

Coach: And, now that this miracle has happened, how will you handle any resistance that might come up?

Client: Tap into that feeling of love and share, and keep sharing my dream.

Coach: How confident are you in your ability to do that?

Client: About a 7 . . . no, maybe an 8, but I really want to be at least a 9.

Coach: As you revisit the feelings of the vision and your 10 out of 10 satisfaction level, how might you move your confidence up one more notch?

Client: Ask for support. Ask my husband to support me. The first step is to share my heart on the camping trip.

Coach: And, is there anything that could stop you from that?

Client: Nope! He deserves to know my dream and I deserve to share it. It is time.

Coach: Yes, speaking of time . . . what value did you create for yourself out of this conversation?

Client: Well, I'm feeling very relaxed right now actually, and I feel very positive about this. I realize I can't keep juggling those balls, that's not the answer, I've got to look at the bigger reality for me and you really helped me put things into perspective. I am excited for who I am becoming. That was really great. Thank you!

Coach: If I was to acknowledge you for the work that you've done here, what would I say to you?

Client: You would say, "You stepped out of your comfort zone and it was worth it."

Coach: Well Emma, you've definitely stepped out of your comfort zone and it *was* worth it. Thank you! It was a pleasure to have the opportunity to work together today.

Client: Thank you. This was awesome.

Continue To Explore Art & Science of Coaching

Book One in the three-book series, *Inner Dynamics,* explores transformational conversations and connects the reader to the inner dynamics of their own inspiration system. The chapters unfold the power of perspective and practice for effectively researching intention and attention. The book contains compelling exercises to explore brain-mind understandings that allow us to connect with our beyond-conscious mind. The book also contains finely-tuned processes to assist yourself and your clients in discovering clear distinctions on the nature of deeper knowing.

This book, Book Two, *Step-by-Step Coaching,* described the stages to transformative conversations. The book systematically took you through the practices and methodologies of powerful coaching conversations. Using examples and exercises you learned to generate these flow conversations in such a way that you boost inspiration and empowerment. Through the maps and methodologies of each chapter, we helped you develop the inner language structures and the action structures that channel goal activation. *Step-by-Step Coaching* was about specific steps, processes, questions, tones, and triggers of inner flow thinking and talking!

Book Three, *Process and Flow,* describes the process and flow of transformational conversations. The book helps readers experientially understand seven kinds of coaching flow states: delight, observation, true value, logical progression, creativity, deep realization, and gratitude. It lays out the power of coaching tools and processes that support people in building new meanings, assessing core values, clarifying choices, and developing visions and futures.

Meet The Authors

The Principal Author: Marilyn Atkinson, PhD.

Marilyn Atkinson Ph.D., the principal author of the three part Art & Science of Coaching Series, conceived and developed many of the concepts, processes and procedures you will meet in the books. An internationally recognized Coach Trainer and Developer, as well as a Consultant to many organizations, a Master NLP trainer, and a Psychologist, Marilyn has spent much of her career working with individuals and organizations to consult, design, and train Solution Focused Coaching and Counseling. She gradually acquired the baseline of highly useful approaches found here and practiced in her courses on four continents.

Marilyn, a Canadian, based in Vancouver, is founder and President of Erickson College International, www.erickson.edu, which trains an International Coach Federation certified program in Coaching. Through her career to date, she has assisted in establishing 14 Erickson Coaching Centers world wide, where she has been teaching solution-focused coaching and counseling since 1985. Marilyn is also known as an NLP and Coaching visionary, leader, and author. Known around the world for her sparkling presence and powerful personal development courses, she is an innovator with impact. Over 30 NLP Institutes in multiple countries use her exercise designs and procedures. Her practical, systemic coaching skills and strategies have been called the Gold Standard of Coaching.

Rae T. Chois

Rae T. Chois is an ICF Master Certified Transformational Coach who works with life long learners to awaken the genius in themselves and others. Rae has over 2500 coaching hours and is widely recognized for her passion and extraordinary talent as a transformational coach, trainer and facilitator engaging large audiences and clients worldwide.

As a trainer with Erickson College International, she has trained and mentored hundreds of coaches across the globe.

Rae is no stranger to the transformational process. As a mother of two young boys, informational entrepreneur, friend, volunteer, athlete, life long learner, etc. Rae has experienced "life's polarity" and learned a lot from the school of hard knocks.

Prior to becoming a master coach and trainer, Rae worked for the Olympic Organizing Committee in Salt Lake City, and in international waters supporting high level communication amongst the 64 countries represented on cruise ships.

Leveraging her international experience, education and radiance as a life long learner, Rae Chois offers a wide range of programs and services including one-on-one Transformational Coaching, group coaching, tele-classes, online live virtual trainings, and in-person trainings.

The book and CD set she co-authored called *The Making Powerful Choices - 30-Day Program* was published in 2005. This "how to" system has since helped hundreds of people across the globe to vividly vision and boldly believe they can and will live the life they love. Her most recent launch is a FREE 28-day meditation and visualization practice called BLISScipline AIM. Visit www.blissicplineaim.com to learn more about this project, which is intended to support people to thrive and help thrive in community through a daily practice.

Suggested Reading

Bateson, G., *Steps to an Ecology of Mind* (Ballantine, 1972).

Beck, Don, *Spiral Dynamics* (Blackwell Publishing, 2005).

Berg, Insoo Kim and Szabo, Peter, *Brief Coaching for Lasting Solutions* (W. W. Norton, 2005).

Brain/Mind Bulletin. Ongoing Periodical (Los Angeles: Interface Press).

Bryne, Rhonda, *The Secret* (Beyond Word Publishing 2006).

Chois, Rae, Chois, Antheny, Heyl, Larrye, and Becket, Cara, *Making Powerful Choices: 30 Day Journey to a Life you Love* (Powerful Choices Publishing, 2005).

Chopra, Deepak *The Seven Spiritual Laws of Success: A Practical Guide to the Fulfillment of Your Dreams* (Amber-Allen, 2007).

de Shazer, Steve, *Keys to Solution in Brief Therapy* (W. W. Norton, 1985).

Demartini, John, *The Breakthrough Experience* (Hay House, 2004).

Dillard, Annie, *Pilgrim at Tinker Creek* (Harper Perennial, 1988).

Dilts, Robert, *Roots of Neuro-Linguistic Programming* (Meta Publications, 1983)

Dooley, Mike, *Notes from the Universe* (Tut, 2003).

Dwoskin, Hale, *The Sedona Method* (Sedona, 2003).

Dyer, Wayne, *Power of Intention: Learning to Co-Create Your World Your Way* (Hay House, 2004)

Gallwey, Tim, *Inner Game of Tennis* ().

Gilligan, Stephen G., *The Legacy of Milton H. Erickson: Selected Papers of Stephen Gilligan* (Zeig, Tucker & Theisen, 2002).

Gordon, David, and Meyers-Anderson, Maribeth, *Phoenix: Therapeutic Patterns of Milton H.Erickson* (M E T a Publications, 1981).

Harris, Bill, *Thresholds of the Mind* (Centerpointe, 2002).

Havens, Ronald A., *The Wisdom of Milton H. Erickson: The Complete Volume* (Crown House, 2005).

David Hawkins, *Power vs. Force: The Hidden Determinants of Human Behaviour* (Hay House, 2002).

Hicks, Jerry and Hicks, Ester, *The Power of Deliberate Intention* (Abraham-Hicks, 2004).

Hicks, Jerry and Hicks, Ester, *Ask and It Is Given. Learning to Manifest your Desires* (Abraham-Hicks, 2004).

Holmes, Ernest, *Creative Mind and Success* (Tarcher, 2004).

James, Tad, *The Secret of Creating Your Future* (Advanced Neuro Dynamics, 1989).

Katie, Byron, *Loving What Is* (Three Rivers Press, 2002).

Oates, Robert, *Permanent Peace: How to Stop Terrorism and War — Now and Forever* (Oates, 2002).

Pearce, Joseph Chilton, *Evolution's End: Claiming the Potential of Our Intelligence* (Harper SanFrancisco, 1992).

Rosenberg, Marshall, *Nonviolent Communication—A Language of Life* (Puddle Dancer, 2003).

Senge, Peter, *The Fifth Discipline* (Century, 1990).

Shapiro, Stephen, *Goal-Free Living—How to Have the Life You Want Now* (Wiley, 2006).

Tolle, Eckhart, *The Power of Now* (Hodder & Stoughton, 1999).

Vitale, Joe, *The Attractor Factor* (Wiley, 2005).

Weakland, J., Fisch, R., Watzlawick, P., and Bodin, A., *Brief Therapy: Focused Problem Resolution* (1974).

Whitworth, Laura, Kimsey-House, Karen, Kimsey-House, Henry, and Sandahl, Phillip, *Co-Active Coaching: New Skills for Coaching People Toward Success in Work and Life* (Davis-Black, 2007)

Williams, Linda V., *Teaching for the Two Sided Mind* (Simon & Shuster, 1983).

Recommended Web Sites

www.coachfederation.org

www.erickson.edu

www.ericksonalberta.ca

www.erickson.no

www.ericksontr.com

www.BLISSciplineAIM.com

www.businesstransformed.com

www.Abraham-Hicks.com

www.tut.com

www.thesecret.tv

www.centerpointe.com

www.peacefulearth.com

ECI Locations

INTERNATIONAL

Erickson College International has live courses in the following locations around the globe. We are adding new locations frequently.

For the most up-to-date information, go to www.erickson.edu and click Locations and Schedules.

Erickson College International Locations Around the World

Australia - Melbourne

Brazil - Sao Paulo

Canada - Multiple Locations
- Calgary
- Edmonton
- Toronto
- Vancouver

China - Beijing

Czech Republic - Prague

Mexico - Mexico City

Norway - Oslo

Poland - Krackow

Russia - Multiple Locations

Turkey - Multiple Locations
- Ankara
- Istanbul

USA - Multiple Locations
- Portland
- Seattle

Art & Science of Coaching: Step-by-Step Coaching

Printed in Great Britain
by Amazon.co.uk, Ltd.,
Marston Gate.